Student Interactive

myView

LITERACY

1

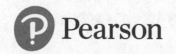

Pearson

Glenview, Illinois   Boston, Massachusetts
Chandler, Arizona   New York, New York

ISBN-13: 978-0-134-90878-6
ISBN-10: 0-134-90878-3

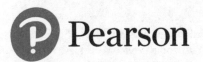

PROGRAM AUTHORS

Julie Coiro, Ph.D.

Jim Cummins, Ph.D.

Pat Cunningham, Ph.D.

Elfrieda Hiebert, Ph.D.

Pamela Mason, Ed.D.

Ernest Morrell, Ph.D.

P. David Pearson, Ph.D.

Frank Serafini, Ph.D.

Alfred Tatum, Ph.D.

Sharon Vaughn, Ph.D.

Judy Wallis, Ed.D.

Lee Wright, Ed.D.

CONTENTS

Making History

Making History

Why is the past important?

▶ **Watch**

"People from the Past" See what you can learn about people from the past.

TURN and TALK What did you learn about people from the past?

PEARSON
realize™
Go ONLINE for all lessons.

- ▶ VIDEO
- ◀) AUDIO
- GAME
- ANNOTATE
- 📖 BOOK
- RESEARCH

Reading Workshop

Reading-Writing Bridge

- Academic Vocabulary
- Read Like a Writer, Write for a Reader
- Spelling • Language and Conventions

Biography

Writing Workshop

- Plan Your Personal Narrative
- Problem and Resolution • What Happens Last
- Edit Verbs • Publish and Celebrate

Personal Narrative

Project-Based Inquiry

Write an Informational Essay　　　　　**Informational Text**

Independent Reading

As you read on your own, compare and contrast the characters in stories or the topics of two informational texts.

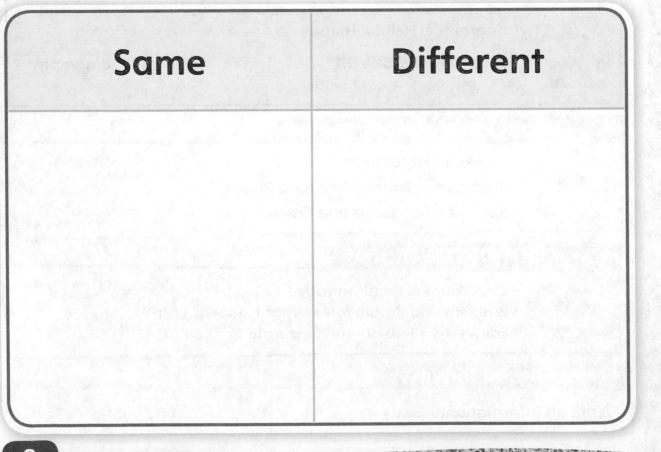

TURN and TALK Use the chart to compare and contrast two books you are reading.

Title _____

Title _____

Same	Different

My Reading Log

Date	Book	Pages Read	Minutes Read	My Ratings
				☺ 😐 ☹
				☺ 😐 ☹
				☺ 😐 ☹
				☺ 😐 ☹
				☺ 😐 ☹

You may wish to use a Reader's Notebook to record and respond to your reading.

Unit Goals

In this unit, you will

- read biographies
- write a personal narrative
- learn about people who made history

MY TURN **Color** the pictures to answer.

I can read biographies.	👍	👎
I can make and use words to read and write narrative nonfiction.	👍	👎
I can write a personal narrative.	👍	👎
I understand why the past is important.	👍	👎

Academic Vocabulary

| record | supply | necessary | experience |

TURN and TALK Read the sentences. With a partner, follow the directions.

Tell about an **experience** in your life.

Record the experience on paper.

Draw a picture to **supply** details about the experience.

Tell why it is **necessary** to record our experiences.

Read Together

Frida Kahlo: Artist

A **time line** is a way to show important events in a person's life.

1907
born in Mexico

1929
married artist Diego Rivera

1925
learned to paint while recovering from a bus accident

became professor of painting at a university **1943**

How do artists of the past help us see the world differently?

TURN and TALK Look at Frida Kahlo's painting. What do you think about her work? Tell your partner how her painting makes you feel.

1954
died in
Mexico

Read Together

Segment and Blend Sounds

SEE and SAY When you segment sounds, you say each sound you hear in a word. Say each picture name. Then segment the sounds. Blend the sounds together to say the picture name again.

r-Controlled Vowel ar

When the vowel **a** is followed by the consonant **r**, it makes the sound you hear in **jar**.

MY TURN Read these words.

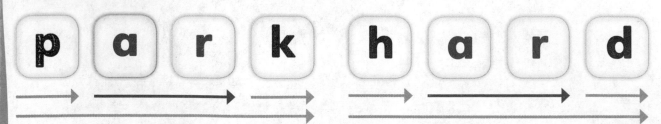

r-Controlled Vowel ar

TURN and TALK Decode these words.

bark	**park**	**dark**	**spark**
car	**far**	**scar**	**star**
art	**cart**	**start**	**chart**
arm	**harm**	**farm**	**charm**

MY TURN Say each picture name. Write **ar** to finish each word. Read each word.

sh __ k   y __ n

r-Controlled Vowel ar

 **MY TURN** Read the sentences. <u>Underline</u> the words with the same vowel sound as **car**.

Bart and Star live on the farm.

Bart will make a card.

Star will do her part to help.

It is not too hard.

Their dog Spark barks at them.

> When **a** is followed by **r**, it makes the sound you hear in **far**.

 **MY TURN** Write a sentence about a card.

My card

Final Sounds

SEE and SAY Listen to the final sounds as you say the picture names. Then say the final sounds.

Inflectional Ending -es, Plural -es

The ending **-es** is added to words that end in **s**, **ch**, **sh**, or **x**.

Adding **-es** to nouns can make plural nouns, or nouns that mean more than one.

Adding **-es** to verbs can show that one person, animal, or thing is doing the action now.

MY TURN Read each word. Highlight the added ending.

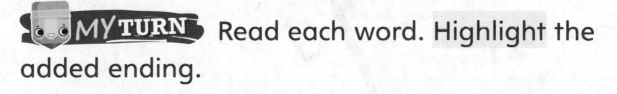

dishes   rushes   catches   buses

My Words to Know

Some words you must identify and practice.

MY TURN Identify and read these words.

| new | found | thank | please | always |

MY TURN Use words from the box to complete the sentences.

Handwriting Print the words clearly.

1. Mark ___found___ a place for his art.

2. He starts ___new___ art with Bart.

3. Mark and Bart ___always___ have fun.

4. They say ___please___ and ___thank___ you.

Inflectional Ending -es, Plural -es

 TURN and **TALK** Decode these word pairs.

bunch	**bunches**	**match**	**matches**
box	**boxes**	**brush**	**brushes**
catch	**catches**	**mix**	**mixes**
rush	**rushes**	**wish**	**wishes**

MY TURN Write each noun as a plural noun. Read the new words.

1. patch _____

2. bench _____

3. fox _____

Inflectional Ending -es, Plural -es

MY TURN Add **-es** to each word. Then read the sentences.

1. Tom and Tiff ride two ___bus_es___.

2. Tom ___dash___ to class.

3. Tiff ___fix___ her homework.

4. Then they eat their ___lunch___.

MY TURN Write a sentence that includes a word with the ending **-es.**

_____

_____

_____

_____

Star Art

Mark is an artist.

He always sets up dishes.

He grabs his new brushes.

Mark starts with a dark blue part.

🔊 AUDIO

Audio with Highlighting

✏ ANNOTATE

Read the story. Highlight the words with the same vowel sound as **far**.

Mark passes his brushes.

Please put stars in the sky.

Barb mixes white on the blue part.

Then she fixes them.

Highlight the three verbs with the ending **-es.**

Mark wipes the <u>brushes</u> and <u>dishes</u>.

Thank you for helping, Barb.

Mark found a place for the art.

<u>Underline</u> the two words with the plural ending **-es**.

My Learning Goal

I can read a biography.

SPOTLIGHT ON GENRE

Biography

A biography is the story of a real person's life written by another person.

Real Person

George Washington was born in Virginia in 1732. He was a farmer and a general. Later he became the first President of the United States.

TURN and TALK Talk about the details of George Washington's life in this biography.

Biography Anchor Chart

informational text

true story of a real person's life

written by someone else

events told in order

Through Georgia's Eyes

Preview Vocabulary

You will read these words in *Through Georgia's Eyes.*

| amaze | memory | wonder | discovers |

Read

Look at the pictures and think about the type of text this is. Make a prediction.

Read to learn about Georgia's life and work.

Ask questions about confusing parts.

Talk about what you learned from the text.

Meet the Author

Rachel Rodríguez always wanted to be a writer. She loves art and nature. She enjoys biking from her San Francisco home through Golden Gate Park.

AUDIO

Audio with Highlighting

ANNOTATE

Through Georgia's Eyes

Rachel Rodríguez
illustrated by Julie Paschkis

27

Georgia's first memory:

She will always remember
these colors and the brightness
of light—light all around.

VOCABULARY IN CONTEXT

<u>Underline</u> the word that helps you understand what the word **memory** means.

Soon Georgia runs and plays games with her brothers and sisters. Her father gives her sweets and plays Irish tunes. Her mother reads stories and cares for the younger children. Everyone works hard on the farm.

Georgia roams the prairie. The trees and land keep her company. Pencil and sketch pad comfort her. She discovers she likes to be alone.

Seasons melt into seasons on her family's farm. Georgia struggles to show on paper what she sees.

   At twelve, she takes painting
lessons. She tells her friend,
"I am going to be an <u>artist</u>."
But in 1899 only boys become
artists. A girl wishing to be
one is scandalous.

Georgia sees life differently. She paints and paints. Hours pass without notice. She wonders if she can achieve her dream.

CLOSE READ

<u>Underline</u> the words that help you understand why Georgia felt she could become an artist.

She walks around a lake
and hikes into the woods.
Everywhere she looks, shapes
hum and sing to her.

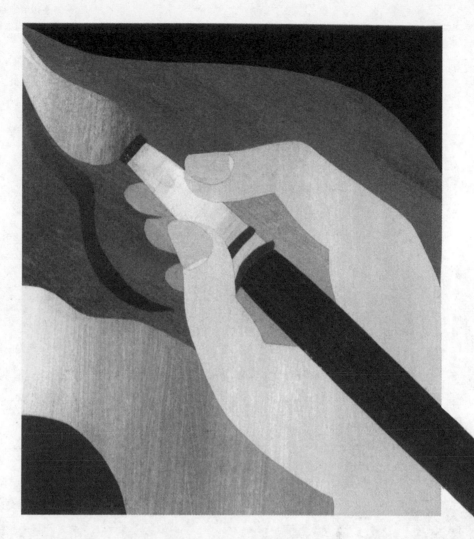

At art school, brushes and canvas become her language. Paint speaks for her. Watercolor and oil are her words.

For a time, Georgia lives in the city. She walks through canyons of concrete. She misses the outdoor world. The sun steals a bite from a skyscraper. The Faraway place—open sky and land—calls her.

CLOSE READ

What question could you ask about these pages? Highlight the words that would answer the question.

The wideness and
wonder of the world
amaze Georgia. She
wants to share this
magic with others.

Flowers delight her. She paints them as <u>giants</u>. People stop to stare. Georgia's flowers make them feel like <u>tiny butterflies,</u> flitting through the universe of her garden.

CLOSE READ

<u>Underline</u> the sentences that tell you how Georgia shares the magic of the world in her flower painting.

She moves to Ghost Ranch in
New Mexico. Red hills, cliffs,
silence, and the Faraway
surround her.

In the desert, she <u>discovers</u> extraordinary things—<u>skulls</u>. The bones don't frighten Georgia. To her, they are alive and strong. Their beauty astounds her.

Georgia expresses feelings in her own way. Words work. But for her, the color blue says it better.
Or red. Or a seashell.
A pale bone.
Sunset.

CLOSE READ

<u>Underline</u> examples of how Georgia expresses her feelings in her own way.

The trees and hills whisper their secrets. They are friends, always there for her.

A canyon calls her. From the bottom at dusk she sees a long line of cows above, black lace against a dusky sky.

She hikes at dawn. She climbs a ridge. The land enchants her.

A range of hills is a mile of elephants with white sand at their feet.

Sometimes her Chow Chow tags along. He hops around rocks and chases antelope. They float ahead of her yelping dog.

Georgia follows them. She breathes in the dawn. A sea of sage covers the plain before a mountain, like waves lapping against a shore.

Sometimes she climbs a ladder to her roof. The moon rises above.

Beneath a giant canvas of inky night and silvery stars, Georgia dreams.

CLOSE READ

What question could you ask about these pages? Highlight the words that would answer the question.

Even now, Georgia can show you the world as she sees it.

Open your eyes . . .

. . . and walk along.

See the colors? Hear the shapes singing?

No need to hurry.

Lean in . . . look closer.

Closer still.

There . . . the wideness
and wonder of the world.

51

Develop Vocabulary

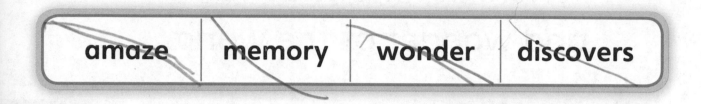 **MY TURN** Complete each sentence with a word from the box. Read the sentences.

amaze	memory	wonder	discovers

1. Georgia has a _memory_ of her mother reading stories.

2. She _discovers_ that she loves art.

3. Georgia believes the world is

   full of _wonder_.

4. The wonder and magic of the

   world _amaze_ her.

Check for Understanding

MY TURN Write the answers to the questions. You can look back at the text.

1. What makes this text a biography?

_____

_____

_____

_____

2. Why does the author write about nature?

_____

_____

_____

_____

3. How does Georgia's early life help her become an artist? Use text evidence.

_____

_____

_____

_____

Describe Connections

A connection is how people, ideas, events, or information in a text are related.

MY TURN Draw lines to make connections. Look back at what you underlined in the text.

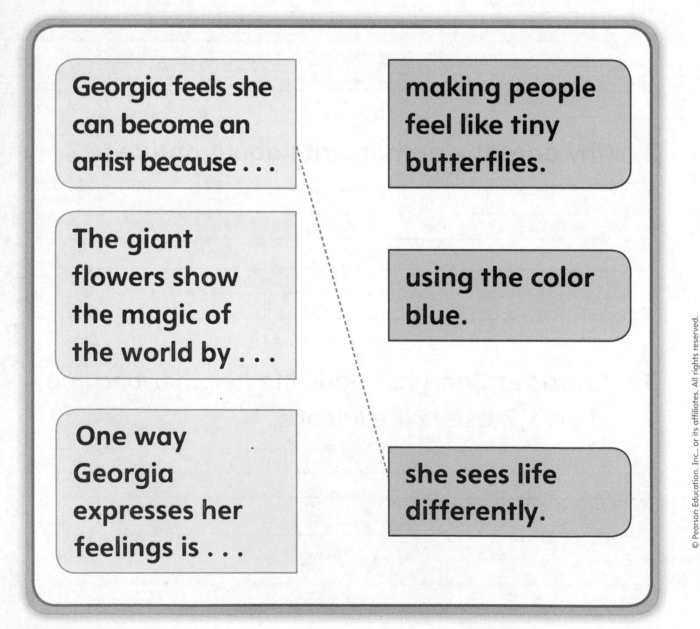

Georgia feels she can become an artist because . . .

making people feel like tiny butterflies.

The giant flowers show the magic of the world by . . .

using the color blue.

One way Georgia expresses her feelings is . . .

she sees life differently.

Ask and Answer Questions

Asking questions before, during, and after reading helps readers better understand what they are reading and learn information.

 **MY TURN** Write a question you can ask about the text. Draw your answer. Use what you highlighted in the text.

Reflect and Share

Talk About It

Retell the story of Georgia O'Keeffe's life. How is her biography similar to and different from another biography you have read?

Retell a Text

When retelling a text, it is important to:

- Use your own words.

- Keep the same meaning as the text.

Use the words on the note to help you retell.

Now retell the text.

First . . . Then . . . Last . . .

Weekly Question

How do artists of the past help us see the world differently?

I can make and use words to read and write narrative nonfiction.

Academic Vocabulary

Related words are connected in some way. They can have similar word parts.

MY TURN Write the word from the box that is related to each set of words.

record	supply	necessary	experience

lesson experiment	supplies materials
experience	
write recording	need necessity

Read Like a Writer, Write for a Reader

Authors choose interesting words or phrases to help readers visualize the text.

> Beneath a giant canvas of inky night and silvery stars, Georgia dreams.

The author uses these phrases to help readers visualize how Georgia sees the world.

TURN and TALK Talk about how the phrases help you visualize the text.

MY TURN Add words to help readers visualize the bear and the cave.

A bear lives in a cave.

_____

_____

_____

_____

Spell r-Controlled ar Words

The letters **ar** spell the vowel sound in **bar**.
A **dictionary** tells the meanings and spellings
of words.

MY TURN Spell the words. Then find four
words in a dictionary.

Spelling Words

car	star	far	card
jar	hard	dark	sharp

car

My Words to Know

always   please

Action Words

Verbs are action words. They can tell about actions in the past, present, or future.

Yesterday I jumped. (past verb tense)
Today I jump. (present verb tense)
Tomorrow I will jump. (future verb tense)

Be sure that when you write a verb, you think about when the action is happening.

MY TURN Edit for correct verb tense. Write the correct verb on the lines.

1. Yesterday Dave will call. _____

2. Jess talked to her mom tomorrow. _____

3. Can we packed our bags right now? _____

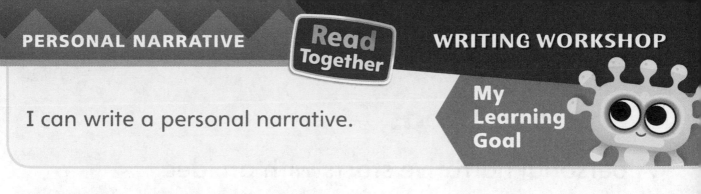

I can write a personal narrative.

My Learning Goal

Personal Narrative

A personal narrative:

- tells about a real event in the author's life
- uses words such as **I**, **my**, and **me**
- tells events and details in time order
- has a sense of closure, or an ending

The Babysitter

My mom called a babysitter last night. An hour later, Mrs. Garcia arrived. I thought it would be boring. But she brought games. We had fun!

Real Event

Author Tells the Story

Closure

Generate Ideas

A personal narrative starts with an idea about a real event.

MY TURN Think about an interesting event in your life. Draw what happens in the boxes.

1.

2.

3.

4.

Plan Your Personal Narrative

MY TURN Plan your personal narrative.

Event

_____

What Happens

_____

Closure

_____

TURN and TALK Use details to describe the people, places, things, and events in your personal narrative.

www.url.here

Martin Luther King, Jr.

A man who changed the world

What He Believed In

- **equality**
- justice
- freedom
- peace

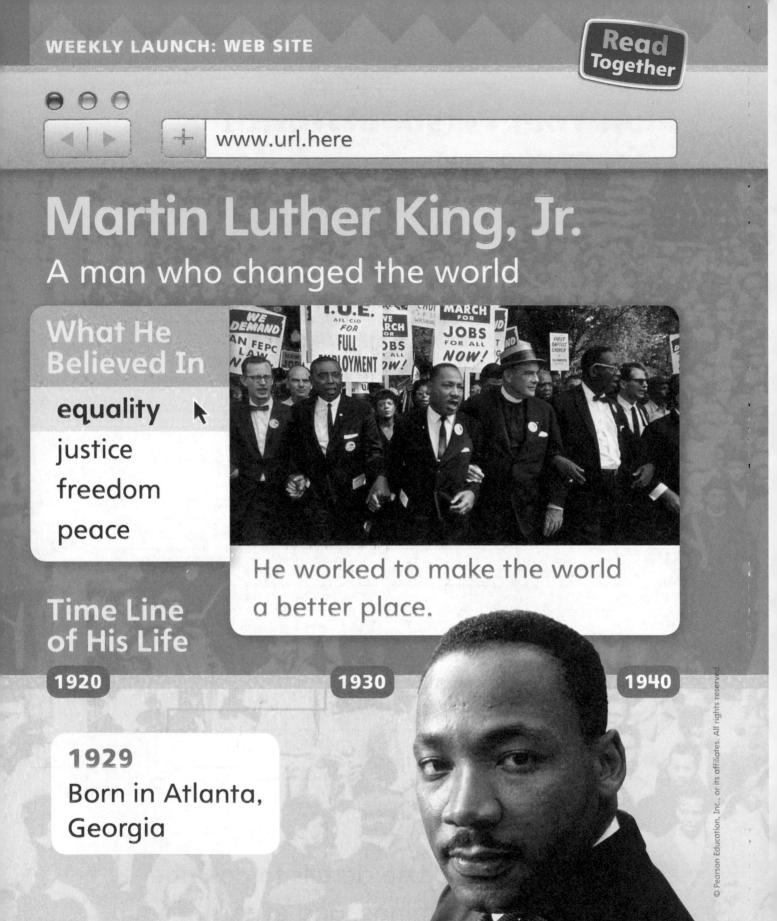

He worked to make the world a better place.

Time Line of His Life

1920 1930 1940

1929
Born in Atlanta, Georgia

Weekly Question

How can a person's actions change the world?

WEEK **2**

Search 🔍

CONTACT US   SHARE   LOG-IN   JOIN

Play this video to listen to his "I Have a Dream" speech.

1963
Led march on Washington; gave "I Have a Dream" speech

1950   **1960**   **1970**

1955
Helped lead bus boycott

1964
Received Nobel Peace Prize

1968
Died in Memphis, Tennessee

MY TURN Circle the features of this Web site, or digital text.

Read Together

Segment and Blend Sounds

 **SEE** and **SAY** When you segment sounds, you say each sound in a word. When you blend sounds, you say all the sounds together. Segment and blend the sounds in each picture name.

r-Controlled Vowels er, ir, ur

The letters **er, ir,** and **ur** all make the vowel sound you hear in **her, dirt,** and **burn.**

MY TURN Read these words.

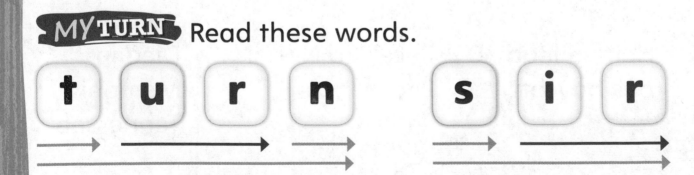

r-Controlled Vowels er, ir, ur

TURN and TALK Decode these words.

fur	**stir**	**perk**
curb	**first**	**verb**

MY TURN Say each picture name.
Circle the word that names each picture.

bird   bid

nest   nurse

fun   fern

ship   shirt

r-Controlled Vowels er, ir, ur

MY TURN Read the sentences. Underline words with r-controlled vowels spelled **er**, **ir**, or **ur**.

The girl sees Bert.

Bert lost his bird.

The girl turns to her left.

Look! The bird is perched on the curb.

Listen for the vowel sound you hear in **fur**.

MY TURN Write a sentence about something else the girl sees. Use a word with **er**, **ir**, or **ur**.

The girl sees

Segment and Blend Sounds

SEE and SAY Say each sound as you name the pictures. Then name the pictures again.

Adding Endings

When a word has a short vowel sound and ends with a consonant, the consonant is doubled before the inflectional ending **-ed** or **-ing** is added.

MY TURN Read the word.

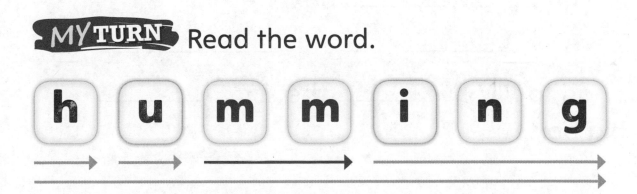

My Words to Know

Some words you must remember and practice.

MY TURN Identify and read these words.

any	pull	very	were	every

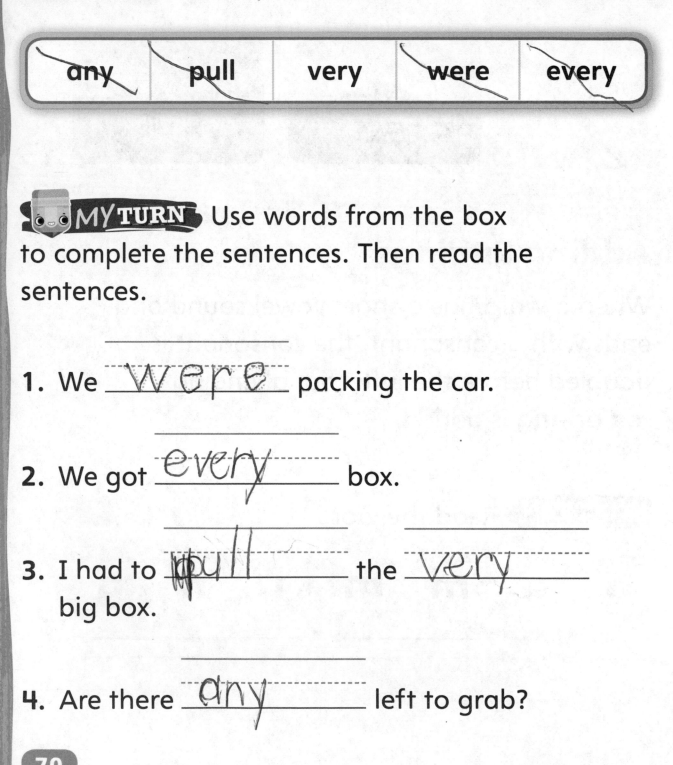

MY TURN Use words from the box to complete the sentences. Then read the sentences.

1. We ___were___ packing the car.

2. We got ___every___ box.

3. I had to ___pull___ the ___very___ big box.

4. Are there ___any___ left to grab?

Adding Endings

TURN and **TALK** Read these words.

batted	**patted**	**patting**
popped	**hopped**	**hopping**
hugged	**tugged**	**tugging**

MY TURN Add the double consonants to the middle of each word.

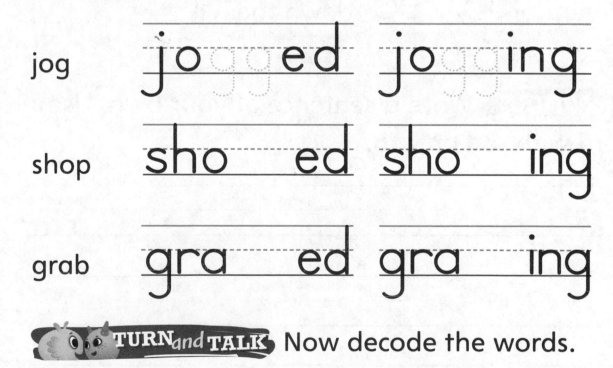

jog   jogged   jogging

shop   sho___ed   sho___ing

grab   gra___ed   gra___ing

TURN and **TALK** Now decode the words.

Adding Endings

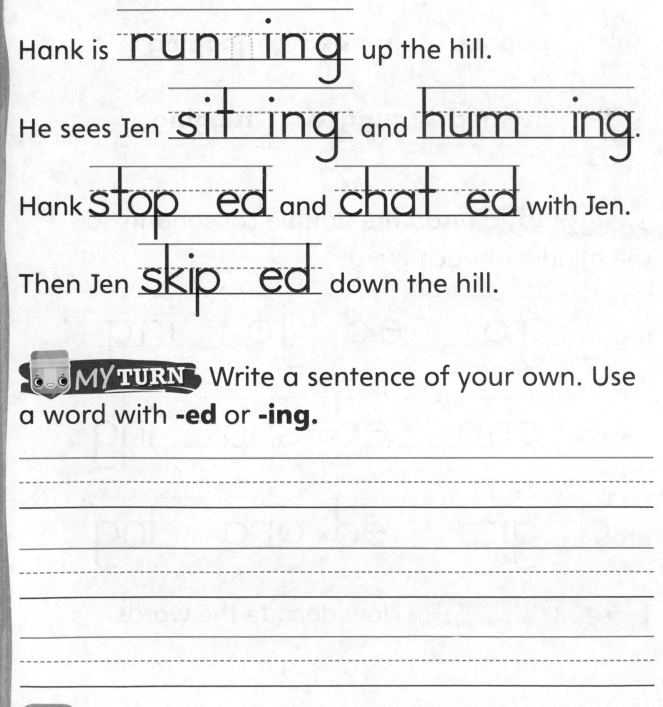

MY TURN Read the sentences. Add the missing consonant to each word that ends in **-ed** or **-ing.**

Hank is __run n ing__ up the hill.

He sees Jen __sit t ing__ and __hum m ing__.

Hank __stop p ed__ and __chat t ed__ with Jen.

Then Jen __skip p ed__ down the hill.

MY TURN Write a sentence of your own. Use a word with **-ed** or **-ing.**

Kurt Can Help

Kurt likes to help every day.

He planted seeds with Mom.

Some dirt got on her shirt.

The seeds turned into ferns.

AUDIO

Audio with Highlighting

ANNOTATE

<u>Underline</u> the seven words with the same vowel sound as **bird.**

Kurt will pull the can to the curb.

There were bits of trash to sort.

Kurt put any plastic in the blue bin.

Highlight the three words with the same vowel sound as **her** spelled **ur.**

Kurt <u>skipped</u> to the park.

It was very dirty.

He gripped his brush.

He rubbed it on the slide.

<u>Underline</u> the three words with inflectional endings.

My Learning Goal

I can read a biography.

SPOTLIGHT ON GENRE

Biography

A biography usually tells events in chronological order, or time order.

Be a Fluent Reader Fluent readers read biographies at an appropriate rate. They read at a speed that is not too fast or too slow. After you read this week's text, practice reading fluently with a partner.

Biography Anchor Chart

Biographies often tell the events of someone's life in the order that they happened.

First

Next

Then

Last

Jackie Robinson

Preview Vocabulary

You will read these words in *Jackie Robinson*.

loved	cheered	admired	allowed

Read

Look at the title and pictures. Ask questions before reading.

Read to understand what this text is about.

Ask questions after reading.

Talk about the text with a partner.

Meet the Author

Wil Mara is the author of over 75 books. He has written stories for both children and adults. Wil even won awards for books he wrote!

Jackie Robinson

By Wil Mara

AUDIO

Audio with Highlighting

ANNOTATE

Do you like to play baseball?

Jack Roosevelt Robinson did. He was so good that he became a Hall of Fame baseball player.

He was born in Cairo, Georgia, on January 31, 1919.

Jackie Robinson loved sports. In college, he was on football, basketball, baseball, and track teams.

CLOSE READ

What did Jackie Robinson love?
Highlight the word.

In 1945, Robinson began playing baseball for a team called the Kansas City Monarchs.

The Monarchs were a team in the Negro League.

CLOSE READ

<u>Underline</u> the phrase that shows the events are told in chronological order, or time order.

There was another baseball league called the Major League. African Americans were not allowed to play in the Major League in those days.

In August of 1945, Robinson met a man named Branch Rickey. Rickey ran a team in the Major League. His team was called the Brooklyn Dodgers.

Rickey asked Robinson to be the first African American to play in the Major League. Robinson said yes.

On April 15, 1947, Jackie Robinson ran onto the field to play first base for the Dodgers.

CLOSE READ

<u>Underline</u> when Jackie Robinson first played for the Dodgers.

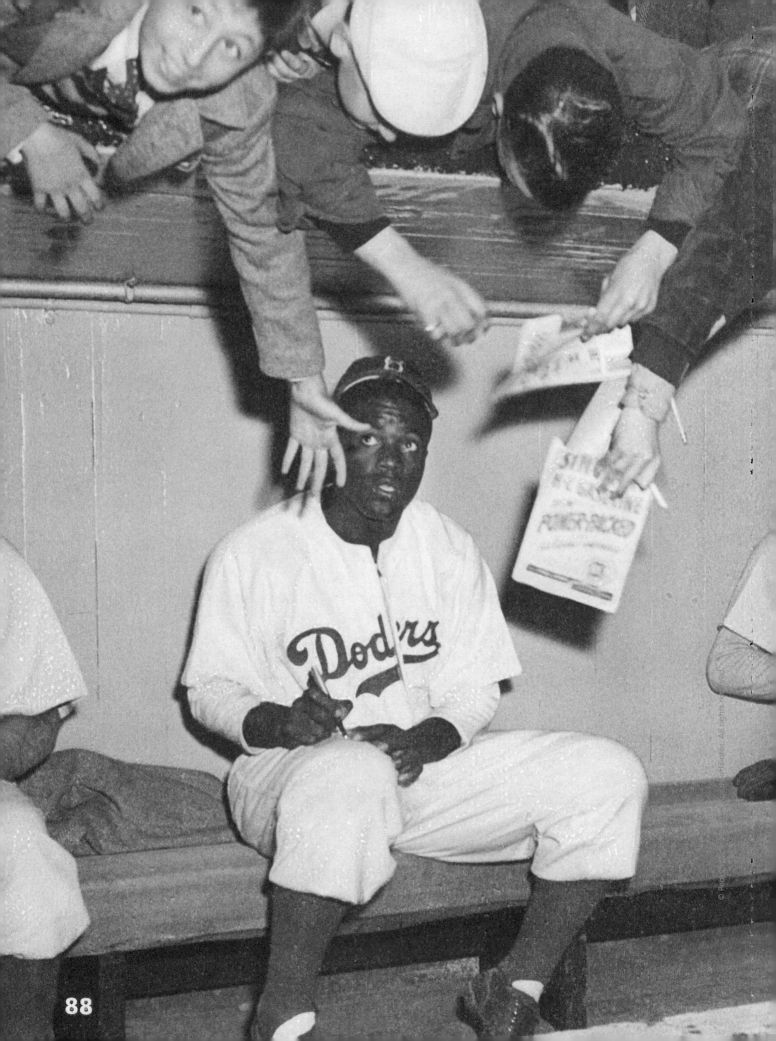

Most baseball fans cheered for Robinson. But some booed. They did not like having an African American play in the Major League.

VOCABULARY IN CONTEXT

Readers can use other words and pictures to help them learn or clarify word meanings. Underline the words that help you figure out what **booed** means.

Robinson kept playing anyway. He worked hard to be a good baseball player.

In his first season, he was Major League's Rookie of the Year. Two seasons later he became the Most Valuable Player.

CLOSE READ

<u>Underline</u> the words and phrases that show the events are told in time order.

Still, many people kept doing and saying mean things to Robinson. They would write nasty letters to him and call him names. Some of these people were his own teammates!

After awhile, Robinson began to stand up for himself. A lot of people admired him for doing this.

CLOSE READ

How does Jackie Robinson react when people are mean to him? Highlight what he does.

Robinson played his last season in 1956. By then, more African Americans were playing in the Major League.

Robinson died on October 24, 1972. He was 53 years old.

"A LIFE IS NOT IMPORTANT EXCEPT IN THE IMPACT IT HAS ON OTHER LIVES."

Jackie Robinson

CLOSE READ

<u>Underline</u> the words and phrases that show the events are told in time order.

Robinson did a great thing with his life. He made a difference. Thanks to Jackie Robinson, African Americans are able to play baseball in the Major League.

FLUENCY

Read pages 92 and 93 aloud with a partner to practice reading at an appropriate rate.

Develop Vocabulary

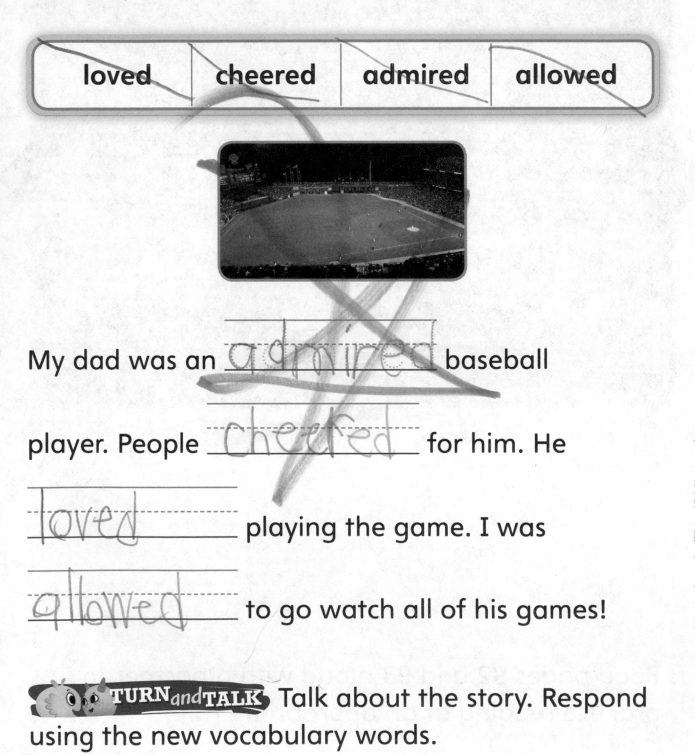

MY TURN Use the vocabulary words to finish the story about baseball.

| loved | cheered | admired | allowed |

My dad was an <u>admired</u> baseball

player. People <u>cheered</u> for him. He

<u>loved</u> playing the game. I was

<u>allowed</u> to go watch all of his games!

TURN and TALK Talk about the story. Respond using the new vocabulary words.

Check for Understanding

MY TURN Write the answers to the questions. You can look back at the text.

1. What details tell you this text is a biography?

_____

_____

_____

_____

2. Why does the author use photographs?

_____

_____

_____

_____

3. How do you think Jackie felt playing baseball? Use text evidence.

_____

_____

_____

_____

Use Text Structure

Text structure is the way information in a text is organized. A biography can be in chronological order, or time order.

 MY TURN Write **1**, **2**, **3**, or **4** to put the events from Jackie Robinson's life in chronological order. Use what you underlined in the text.

_____ Jackie was Major League's Rookie of the Year.

_____ Jackie played his final season.

_____ Jackie plays first base for the Dodgers.

_____ Jackie began playing baseball for the Monarchs.

Create New Understandings

Readers can synthesize, or combine, information they read in a text to learn something new.

MY TURN What new understanding can you come up with about why Jackie Robinson stood up for himself? Look back at what you highlighted in the text.

Reflect and Share

Write to Sources

You read a biography of Jackie Robinson. On a separate sheet of paper, write about another biography you have read. Use text evidence to show how the biographies are similar or different.

Use Text Evidence

Text evidence is details from the text that support your ideas. When writing about texts, you should:

- Find examples in the text.
- Explain how the examples support your ideas.

Weekly Question

How can a person's actions change the world?

I can make and use words to read and write narrative nonfiction.

Academic Vocabulary

Antonyms are words that have opposite meanings.

MY TURN Read the sentences. Then write the antonym of each underlined word.

keep	extra	delete

1. Jan got the <u>necessary</u> books.

   Jan got the _____extra_____ books.

2. Bart will <u>give</u> the paper.

   Bart will _____ the paper.

3. Jon can <u>save</u> the notes.

   Jon can _____ the notes.

Read Like a Writer, Write for a Reader

Authors use graphic features, such as photos, to help readers understand more about the text.

In August of 1945, Robinson met a man named Branch Rickey.

The author uses the photo to show Branch Rickey.

TURN and TALK Choose a photo from the text and tell why the author uses it.

MY TURN Write about a person you know. Draw a picture of the person.

_____

- -

_____

- -

_____

Spell r-Controlled er, ir, ur Words

The letters **er**, **ir**, and **ur** spell the vowel sound in **fern**, **stir**, and **curb**.

MY TURN Sort and spell the words.

Spelling Words			
her	girl	bird	term
dirt	hurt	turn	birth

ir

girl

_____

_____

_____

ur

_____

_____

er

_____

_____

_____

My Words to Know

were   very

_____

_____

_____

Past Verb Tense

Verbs in the past tense tell about something that happened before. These verbs often have the ending **-ed**.

She **worked** hard to fix the town.

I **helped** her clean the streets.

MY TURN Edit the sentences. Change the present tense verbs to past tense verbs.

1. Rex and Jen wash the dishes.

Rex and Jen ____washed____ the dishes.

2. They clean up the trash.

They _____ up the trash.

3. They plant trees.

They _____ trees.

Setting

The **setting** is where and when an event takes place. The setting in a personal narrative is a real place in the author's life.

MY TURN Read the passage. <u>Underline</u> the words that describe the setting.

Last Saturday, Ben and I walked to the park. There were lots of kids there. We played basketball all morning until it was time for lunch.

MY TURN Add words and phrases to your personal narrative that describe the setting.

The Narrator: You

You are the narrator, or person telling the events, in your personal narrative. The words **I** and **me** are used in personal narratives to show that the author is telling the events.

MY TURN Write a sentence that could be a topic of a personal narrative. Use **I** or **me** to show that you are the narrator. Then draw yourself in that story.

_____

- -

_____

- -

_____

MY TURN Compose a personal narrative with you as the person telling the events.

Problem and Resolution

A personal narrative can have a problem and resolution. The **problem** is what needs to be solved. The **resolution** is the outcome.

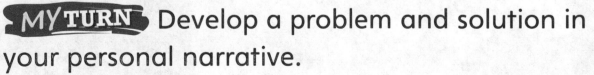 **MY TURN** Use an event from your life to complete this chart. Use specific and relevant details.

Problem

_____

- -

_____

- -

_____

Resolution

_____

- -

_____

- -

_____

MY TURN Develop a problem and solution in your personal narrative.

Read Together

Technology in Our Lives

Virtual Reality

Virtual reality, or VR, lets people see new worlds! You can visit Mars, play inside a video game, or be a part of a movie!

Self-Driving Cars

Some cars can take people to places safely without anyone needing to drive.

3D Printers

3D printers can build toys and cars. These printers can use ingredients to make food!

TURN *and* **TALK** What technology do you think is the most interesting?

Read Together

Final Sounds

SEE and SAY Look at the first big elephant. Compare the sizes of the elephants. Use the final sounds **er** and **est**.

Comparative Endings

The **-er** ending can be added to an adjective to compare two things.

The **-est** ending can be added to an adjective to compare three or more things.

MY TURN Read each word.

soft   softer   softest

Comparative Endings

TURN and TALK Read these words.

hard	**harder**	**hardest**
fast	**faster**	**fastest**

MY TURN Read the first word. Add **-er** or **-est** to compare the pictures in each set.

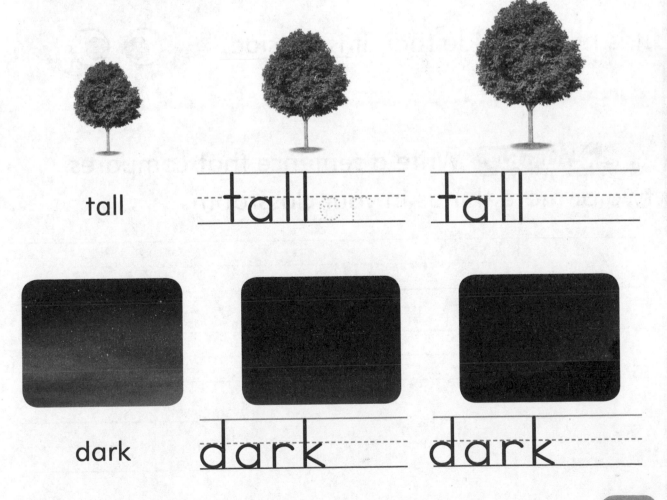

tall   tall____   tall

dark   dark   dark

Comparative Endings

MY TURN Read each sentence. <u>Underline</u> the word that compares.

The bird is <u>smaller</u> than the cat.

Barb is the smartest one in the class.

Who is the shortest one in your class?

It is hotter inside than it is outside.

> The ending **-er** compares two things. The ending **-est** compares three or more things.

MY TURN Write a sentence that compares two or more things in your classroom.

_____

_____

_____

_____

Final Sounds

 SEE and SAY Say each sound as you name each picture. Then say the name of each picture again. Tell the final sound in each picture name.

Trigraph dge

Sometimes three letters make one sound, such as the letters dge in edge.

MY TURN Read the word.

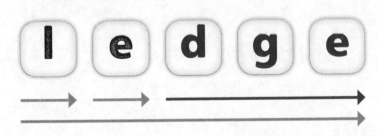

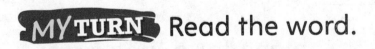

My Words to Know

Some words you must remember and practice.

MY TURN Read these words.

| our | away | light | never | pretty |

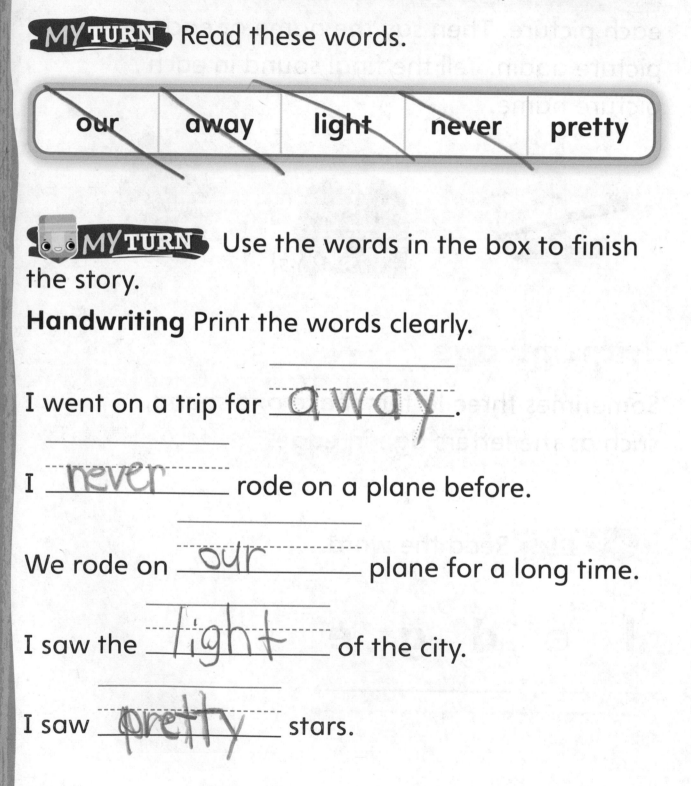

MY TURN Use the words in the box to finish the story.

Handwriting Print the words clearly.

I went on a trip far ___away___.

I ___never___ rode on a plane before.

We rode on ___our___ plane for a long time.

I saw the ___light___ of the city.

I saw ___pretty___ stars.

Trigraph dge

TURN and TALK Decode the words.

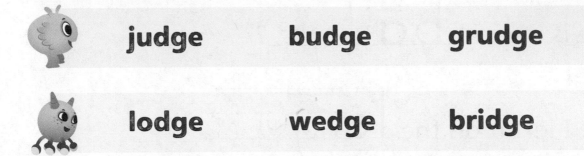

| judge | budge | grudge |

| lodge | wedge | bridge |

MY TURN Add **dge** to finish the words. Then draw a line from each word to its picture.

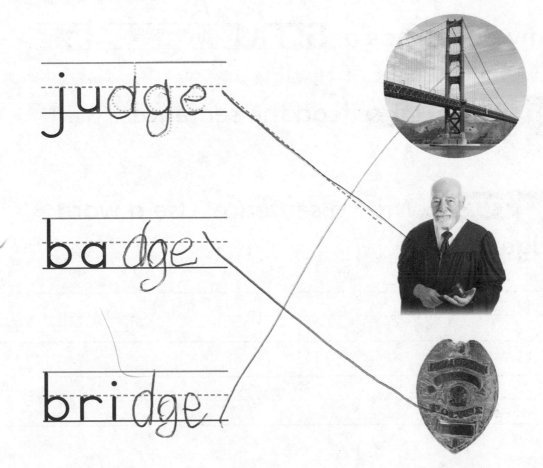

judge

ba*dge*

bri*dge*

Trigraph dge

MY TURN Write **dge** to finish the words.

Where is my red ba**dge** ?

I think I left it on the le**dge** .

No, it is on the e**dge** of my desk.

Now my badge has a smu**dge** .

TURN and TALK Read the sentences.

MY TURN Write a sentence. Use a word with **dge.**

Cars by Bob

Bob made our newest car.

The car is light blue.

It is the fastest one I know.

We can go places far away.

AUDIO

Audio with Highlighting

ANNOTATE

Highlight the two words with endings that compare.

Bob has a name <u>badge</u>.

He works hard to make pretty cars.

They never have a <u>smudge</u>.

You be the <u>judge</u>!

<u>Underline</u> the three words with the same final sound as **edge**.

His cars have an edge.

They help Dad drive smarter.

We turn to dodge bad things.

Can Bob make safe cars faster?

Highlight the two words with endings that compare.

Read Together

I can read about people who have made history.

Historical Fiction

Historical fiction is a made-up story that takes place in a real setting in the past. It has a topic, or what the text is all about.

The Trip

Topic — Oscar and his family are traveling out west in a covered wagon. It is a long trip.

"We must stop to make a fire and rest," Dad says.

 TURN and TALK Talk about how historical fiction is similar to and different from biographies.

Historical Fiction Anchor Chart

Setting
real time period and place in the past

Characters
made-up characters

Details
facts from history

Before the Railroad Came

Preview Vocabulary

You will read these words in *Before the Railroad Came*.

drive	ranch	cattle	railroad

Read

Read to understand the big ideas in the text.

Look at the pictures to help clarify what is happening.

Ask questions during and after reading.

Talk about the big ideas with a partner.

Meet *the* Author

Jerry Craft is an author and illustrator. He wrote a superhero book with his two sons. Jerry also makes a newspaper comic strip and loves to visit schools.

BEFORE THE RAILROAD CAME

written by Jerry Craft
illustrated by Doris Ettlinger

AUDIO
Audio with Highlighting
ANNOTATE

My name is Samuel. I'm seven years old, and I live on a <u>ranch</u> in Texas. Working on a ranch is hard work, but it used to be much harder.

Before the railroad came, Dad had to take long trips to get our cattle to the <u>market</u>. Sometimes it was weeks before he returned home.

CLOSE READ

<u>Underline</u> the details that help you figure out the topic and theme, or big idea.

Before the railroad came,
my older brothers got to go
with Dad on these trips. Dad
promised me that he would
take me with him when I got
old enough.

But then the railroad came. Now Dad and my brothers load our cattle onto railroad cars. The train takes the cattle all the way to the market.

"I know you wanted to go on a cattle drive," Dad said, "but the railroad is good for us. It makes our lives a lot easier."

"By the way," Dad said. "I have a surprise that may make you change your mind about the railroad."

"What kind of surprise?" I asked.

CLOSE READ

Highlight how the railroad changed the way people lived.

"We're all going to take the train to Dallas," Dad said. "We'll visit Grandma and Grandpa there."

I had never been to Dallas before!

Before the railroad came, I could never imagine visiting Dallas. But we're on our way there right now. I can hardly wait to get there!

CLOSE READ

Highlight how the railroad changed Samuel's life.

Develop Vocabulary

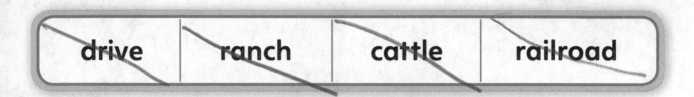 **MY TURN** Use the words in the box to finish the sentences.

drive	ranch	cattle	railroad

Samuel lives on a __ranch__ in Texas.

He wants to go on a cattle __drive__ with his dad.

The __railroad__ changes his plans.

Now they load the __cattle__ on the railroad cars.

Check for Understanding

 **MY TURN** Write the answers to the questions. You can look back at the text.

1. How can you tell this text is historical fiction?

_____

_____

_____

2. Why does the author repeat the phrase "**Before the railroad came**"?

_____

_____

_____

3. Why does Samuel like trains by the end? Use text evidence.

_____

_____

_____

135

Determine Theme

The **theme** is the message or big idea of a text. The **topic,** or what a text is all about, can help you figure out the theme. When you discuss topics and determine theme, use text evidence to support what you are saying.

MY TURN What is the theme of *Before the Railroad Came?* Look back at what you underlined in the text.

The theme of *Before the Railroad Came* is

_____

_____

_____

_____

_____

_____

TURN and TALK Discuss the topic of the text. How does the topic help you figure out the theme?

Make Connections

Readers make connections to the big ideas in a text. They can connect the big ideas to their lives, other texts they have read, or to the world around them.

 **MY TURN** Write and draw about a connection you can make to the big idea of *Before the Railroad Came*. Look back at what you highlighted in the text.

_____

- -

_____

- -

_____

- -

_____

Reflect and Share

Talk About It

What is your opinion of Samuel? How is he like other characters you have read about? How is he different?

Tell an Opinion

When telling an opinion, it is important to:

◎ Say what you think or believe.

◎ Use a reason to support your opinion.

Use the words on the note to help you.

Now tell your opinion.

I think . . .
because . . .

Weekly Question

How can technology change the world?

I can make and use words to connect reading and writing.

My Learning Goal

Academic Vocabulary

Context clues are words or pictures that help you learn or clarify the meaning of an unknown word.

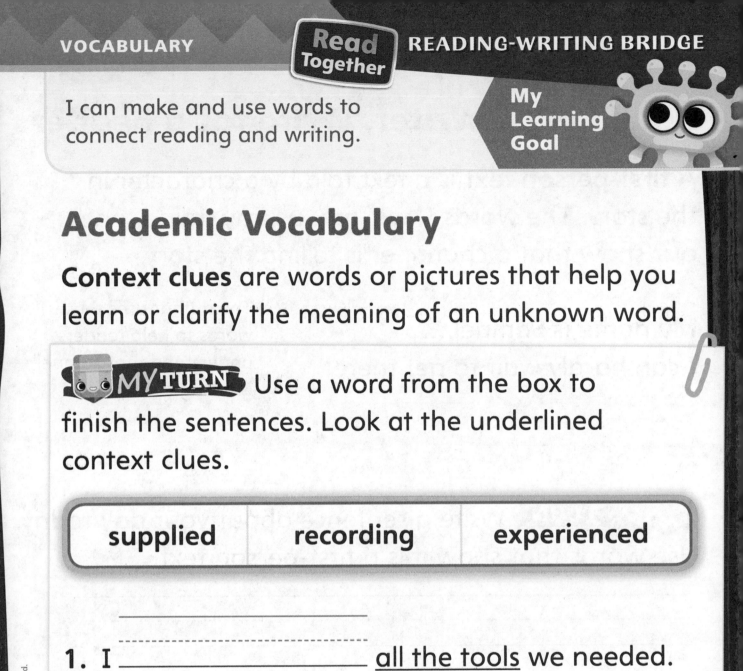

MY TURN Use a word from the box to finish the sentences. Look at the underlined context clues.

supplied	recording	experienced

1. I _____ all the <u>tools</u> we needed.

2. We made a _____ of the <u>song</u>.

3. I _____ a <u>fun ride on a train</u>.

Read Like a Writer, Write for a Reader

A **first-person text** is a text told by a character in the story. The words **I, we, me, us, my, mine,** and **our** show that a character is telling the story.

My name is Samuel....
I can hardly wait to get there!

The author uses these words to help readers understand that Samuel is telling the story.

 MY TURN Write a sentence about your day today. Use words that show it is a first-person text.

_____

_____

_____

_____

_____

Spell Words That Compare

Words that compare two things end with **-er**.
Words that compare three or more end with **-est**.

MY TURN Spell and sort the words.

Spelling Words

faster	fastest	slow	slower
slowest	short	shorter	shortest

Does Not Compare

slow
_____

_____

Compares Three or More

_____

_____

_____

_____

Compares Two

_____

_____

_____

My Words to Know

away   pretty

_____

_____

Verbs

A **verb** is a word that shows action. **Future verb tense** tells about something that will happen later. The word **will** comes before the verb.

I **will read** about the history of planes.
I **will go** to a history museum.

MY TURN Underline the verbs.
Then edit the verbs to be in the future verb tense.

1. I walk to the train tomorrow.

    will walk

2. I ride the train home later.

3. Sam and Dad tell me about the trip.

I can write a personal narrative.

What Happens First

A personal narrative tells events in the order that they happen. It begins with what happens first. Authors use words or phrases such as **first**, **at first**, and **in the beginning** to tell what happens first.

MY TURN Write about what happens first when you get to school.

_____

- -

_____

- -

_____

- -

_____

MY TURN Develop a draft of your personal narrative that tells what happens first.

What Happens Next

Authors use words such as **next, later,** and **then** to tell what happens next in their personal narratives. They revise to add details to the words to tell more about the event.

MY TURN Read the sentence. Then write about what happens next.

I got home from school.

_____

_____

_____

_____

_____

_____

_____

MY TURN Revise your personal narrative by adding details to the words.

What Happens Last

What happens last in a personal narrative provides a sense of closure. Authors use words that show the event is the last to happen.

First, Greg and I rode our bikes to school. Then we had to ride on the grass. **In the end**, I fell off my bike! But I was fine.

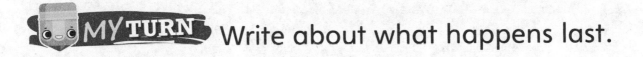 Write about what happens last.

What a day! First, I woke up late. Then I couldn't find my backpack. When I got to school,

_____

- -

_____

- -

_____

- -

_____

MY TURN Develop your personal narrative draft by writing about what happens last.

What Is America?

America is the land of the free.

America is the people I see.

America is the country I roam.

America is the place I call home.

Why is it important to learn about our country's past?

 **MY TURN** When you interact with a text, you read and respond to it in a way that helps you understand it. Interact with this text by drawing what America is to you.

Middle and Final Sounds

SEE and SAY Say each sound as you name each picture. Then say each picture name again.

Diphthongs ow, ou

The **ou** sound can be spelled **ow**, as in **cow**.
The **ou** sound can be spelled **ou**, as in **cloud**.

MY TURN Read the words.

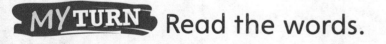

Diphthongs ow, ou

 **TURN and TALK** Decode these words
with a partner.

town	**down**	**brown**
mouse	**house**	**blouse**

MY TURN Say the picture name.
<u>Underline</u> the word that names the picture.

<u>couch</u>   count   <u>cow</u>   cot

<u>owl</u>   ox   close   <u>cloud</u>

Diphthongs ow, ou

MY TURN Write a word from the box to finish the sentences. Then read the sentences.

now	loud	down	crowd	round

Sam will run the ___round___ track.

The _____ is up and _____ .

_____ they are _____ !

MY TURN Write a sentence that includes a word with **ow** or **ou**.

_____

_____

_____

Different Sounds

 **SEE and SAY** You can listen for sounds that are alike and different. Say each picture name. Listen to the middle sound. Tell which picture has the long **a** sound. Tell which picture has the short **a** sound.

Vowel Digraphs ai, ay

The long **a** sound can be spelled **ai**, as in **main**. The long **a** sound can be spelled **ay**, as in **may**.

MY TURN Read the words.

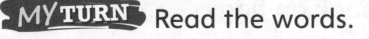

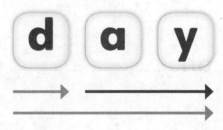

My Words to Know

Some words you must remember and practice.

MY TURN Read these words.

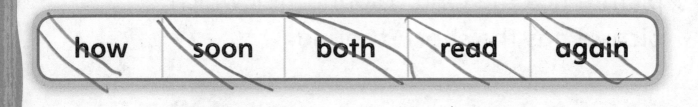

| how | soon | both | read | again |

MY TURN Write words from the box to complete the sentences. Read the sentences.

1. We can raise the flag ___soon___.

2. ___How___ do we raise a flag ___again___?

3. ___Read___ the book on flags.

4. Can ___both___ of you find the flag?

Vowel Digraphs ai, ay

TURN and TALK Decode these words with a partner.

rain	main	chain
may	day	hay
pay	play	stay
mail	nail	sail

MY TURN Name the pictures. <u>Underline</u> the letters in each name that make the long **a** sound.

train

snail

hay

Vowel Digraphs ai, ay

MY TURN Read the sentences. <u>Underline</u> the words with the long **a** sound.

Jay and Ray wait in line.

Ray paid for their train passes.

Jay and Ray look for their train.

"It is that way!" Jay and Ray say.

Listen for the long **a** sound spelled **ai** and **ay**.

MY TURN Write a new sentence about Jay and Ray. Use a word with the long **a** sound.

Jay and Ray

Raise the Flag

Gail will raise the flag again.

It is the main part of the day!

The class waits.

They say the pledge out loud.

AUDIO

Audio with Highlighting

ANNOTATE

Read the story. Highlight the seven words with the long **a** sound spelled **ai** or **ay**.

Now what will they do?

Soon they will count.

They will use brown paint.

They may read one story.

Underline the three words with the
same vowel sound as **cow**.

The flag must come down.

How will Gail take it down?

No one makes a sound.

Both Gail and the class like their flag.

Highlight the four words with the same vowel sound as **cow**.

My Learning Goal

I can read about people who have made history.

Informational Text

Informational text has supporting evidence, or details, that tell about a main, or central, idea. It can have features, such as labels.

torch

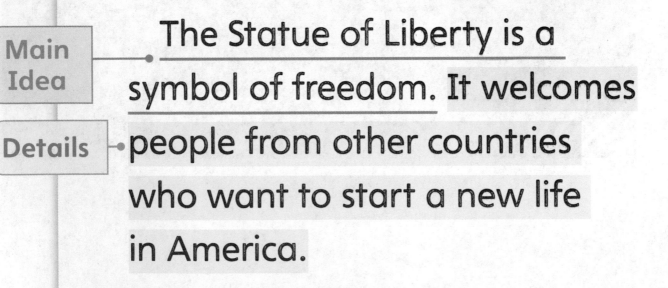

Main Idea

Details

The Statue of Liberty is a symbol of freedom. It welcomes people from other countries who want to start a new life in America.

TURN and TALK How are biography and informational text alike and different?

Informational Text Anchor Chart

Details

Main Idea

from What Is the Story of Our Flag?

Preview Vocabulary

You will read these words in *What Is the Story of Our Flag?*

| stars | field |

Read and Compare

Look through the text. Make a prediction.

Read to find the most important ideas.

Ask questions to clarify information.

Compare this text to *The First American Flag*.

Meet the Author

Janice Behrens writes books for children. She lives in New York City with her family. Janice learned how to fold a flag when she was a kid.

title

from **What Is the Story of Our Flag?**

by Janice Behrens

AUDIO

Audio with Highlighting

ANNOTATE

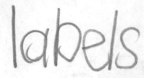

stripes

stars

Our flag is red, white, and blue. It has **stars** and **stripes**. But did you know that the American flag has not always looked the same?

When our country was new, the leaders decided we needed a flag. Back then, there were only 13 **states**. The first flag had a star and a stripe for each state.

states

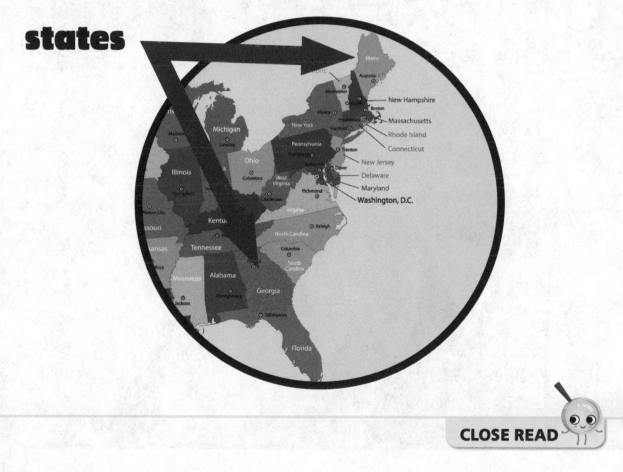

CLOSE READ

Underline the sentence that describes the first flag.

The first flag had 13 stars and 13 stripes,
like this one. Count them!

Who made the first flag?
No one knows for sure.
Some people think it was
a **seamstress** who lived in
Philadelphia. Her name was
Betsy Ross.

seamstress

sew

VOCABULARY IN CONTEXT

What does the word **seamstress** mean? What
part of the picture helps you figure it out?

field

Over the years, new states joined the country. Stars were added to the blue field. Sometimes the stars were in a circle. Other times they were in rows.

Sometimes stripes were added too.

Our flag today has 50 stars. There is one for each state. It has 13 stripes, for the first 13 states. When people see the flag, they think of our country.

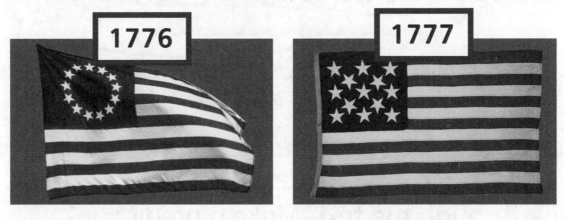

1776

1777

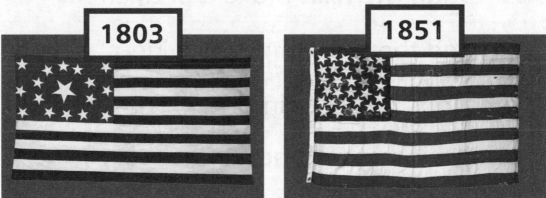

1803

1851

Can you count the stars and stripes on these old flags?

CLOSE READ

Highlight the details that tell how the flag has changed over time.

from The First American Flag

Preview Vocabulary

You will read these words in *The First American Flag*.

patch	stripes

Read and Compare

Look through the text. Make a prediction.

Read to find the most important ideas.

Ask questions to clarify information.

Compare this text to *What Is the Story of Our Flag?*

Meet *the* Illustrator

Siri Weber Feeney makes pictures for children's books. She enjoys illustrating people of different cultures and turning history into art.

from # The First American Flag

by Kathy Allen
illustrated by Siri Weber Feeney

AUDIO

Audio with Highlighting

ANNOTATE

Many people believe a man named Francis Hopkinson designed the first U.S. flag.

His flag had 13 red and white stripes. The corner had 13 six-pointed stars on a patch of blue.

On June 14, 1777, "Hopkinson's flag" became the first flag of the United States. It was called the Stars and Stripes.

As states were added to the country, stars and stripes were added to the flag. By 1795, the flag had 15 stars and 15 stripes.

By 1818, there were 20 states.

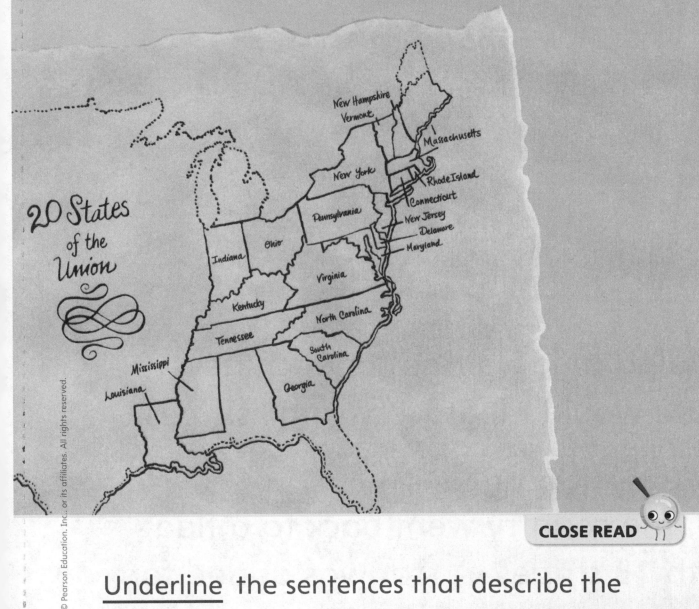

20 States of the Union

New Hampshire
Vermont
Massachusetts
New York
Rhode Island
Connecticut
New Jersey
Delaware
Maryland
Pennsylvania
Indiana
Ohio
Virginia
Kentucky
North Carolina
Tennessee
South Carolina
Mississippi
Georgia
Louisiana

CLOSE READ

<u>Underline</u> the sentences that describe the first flag.

Adding a new stripe for each new state would mean very small stripes or a very tall flag!

So, the country went back to a flag with 13 stripes. A star was added for each new state.

By 1959, there were 50 states. The flag got its 50th star on July 4, 1960. The star stands for the state of Hawaii.

The flag of the United States has come a long way.

CLOSE READ

Highlight the details that describe how the flag has changed over time.

Develop Vocabulary

MY TURN Look at the picture. Write the word that fits each label.

stars	field	patch	stripes

the _field_, or

_____, of blue

one of the 50

_____

the 13 red and white

_____

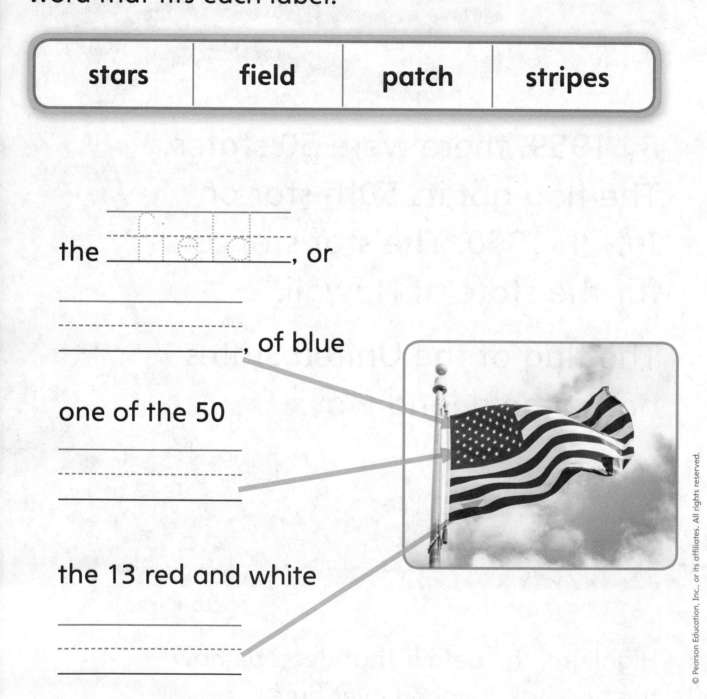

Check for Understanding

MY TURN Write the answer to each question. You can look back at the texts.

1. How does the topic of each text help you know these are informational texts?

_____

_____

----

2. Why does the author use bold words?

_____

_____

----

3. How are Betsy Ross and Francis Hopkinson alike? Use text evidence.

_____

_____

Compare and Contrast Texts

A **topic** is what a text is about. Readers **compare** texts to tell how they are alike. Readers **contrast** texts to tell how they are different.

MY TURN What is the topic of both texts? Look back at what you underlined to help you answer the question.

Both texts are about _____

_____

_____

How are the two texts different?

_____

_____

_____

_____

Find Important Details

Details are the most important pieces of information about a main idea. Details can help readers compare and contrast two texts.

MY TURN Draw the most important details from the texts. Look back at what you highlighted in both texts.

TURN and TALK Talk about how the details in the texts are alike and different.

Reflect and Share

Talk About It

You read two texts about our country's past. How are the two texts alike? Describe a personal connection you can make to the texts.

Make Connections

When describing personal connections, think about:

- Your experiences.
- Feelings you have had.
- Things you have seen.

One time, I . . .

Use these words on the note to help you.

Now describe a personal connection.

Weekly Question

Why is it important to learn about our country's past?

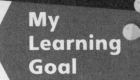

I can make and use words to connect reading and writing.

My Learning Goal

Academic Vocabulary

Word parts can be added to some words. These words become new words with different meanings.

The word part **re-** means "**again.**"

The word part **un-** means "**not.**"

The word part **-able** means "**able to.**"

MY TURN Finish each sentence.

Unnecessary means " _____not_____ necessary."

Recordable means " _____ record."

Resupply means "to supply _____."

Read Like a Writer, Write for a Reader

Authors use print features, such as bold text and labels, to help readers find important details.

Some people think it was a **seamstress** who lived in Philadelphia.

The author uses bold text and a label.

TURN and **TALK** Find a print feature in the text and talk about why the author uses it.

MY TURN Write a label for the picture.

_____

_____

_____

Spell Words with Diphthongs ow, ou

The **ou** sound is spelled **ow** in **town** and **ou** in **cloud.** When you alphabetize, you put a series, or list, of words in order of the alphabet.

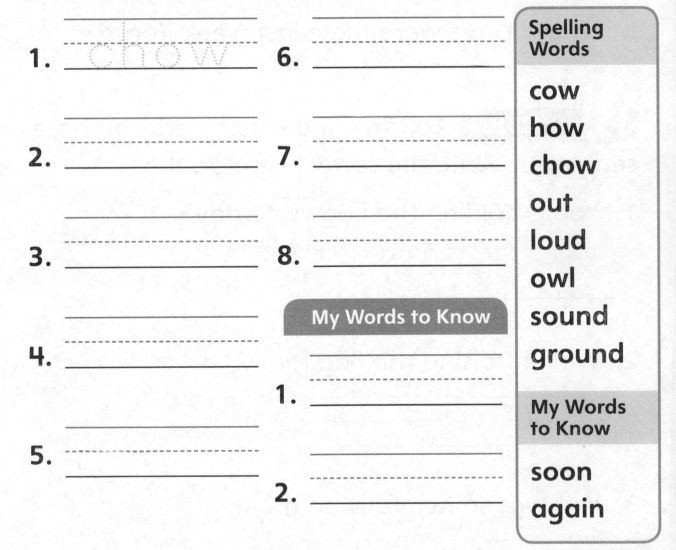

MY TURN Alphabetize the words in each list to the second letter.

1. chow

2.

3.

4.

5.

6.

7.

8.

My Words to Know

1.

2.

Spelling Words

cow

how

chow

out

loud

owl

sound

ground

My Words to Know

soon

again

Verbs

The words **am**, **are**, **is**, **was**, and **were** are kinds of verbs. They do not show action. **Am, are**, and **is** are in the present tense. **Was** and **were** are in the past tense.

I **am** at the mall now. (present)

Mike and Dave **were** there last week. (past)

MY TURN Edit the underlined verbs in these sentences. Write the correct verb on the line.

1. You <u>is</u> holding the flag yesterday.

_____

~~were~~

_____

2. We <u>am</u> raising the flag today.

_____

_____

3. You <u>was</u> so helpful with the flag!

_____

_____

I can write a personal narrative.

My Learning Goal

Edit for Capitalization

Authors always capitalize the beginning of sentences, the pronoun **I**, the days, the months, and the names of people.

The flag will go up on **S**unday.

I will help **S**am in **S**eptember.

MY TURN Edit for capital letters. Write the correct word.

1. Jim and i read a new book. _____

2. the book is about flags. _____

3. We need it on friday. _____

MY TURN Edit your personal narrative for capital letters.

Edit Punctuation Marks

Sentence Type	Punctuation Mark	Example
declarative sentence	period	I can come to the park.
interrogative sentence	question mark	Where are you?
exclamatory sentence	exclamation mark	Watch out!

MY TURN Edit the punctuation marks.

The best part of our trip was the parade _____ .

It was so much fun to watch _____

The spinning flag was amazing _____

Do you want to know more _____

MY TURN Edit the punctuation marks in your personal narrative.

Edit Verbs

Past Tense	add -ed	I **walked** to school.

| Present Tense | one subject: add -s | Jane **walks**. |
| | two or more subjects: do not add -s | Jane and Tim **ride**. |

| Future Tense | add **will** before verb | I **will walk** to school. |

MY TURN Underline the verbs. Edit the verb tense.

1. Jack <u>bring</u> the flag tomorrow. _will bring_

2. We pick the flag up last time. _____

3. We looks at the flag with pride. _____

MY TURN Edit the verbs in your personal narrative.

Read Together

Helpful Heroes

Clara Barton

Clara was a nurse. She started the American Red Cross. The Red Cross cares for people who need help.

Booker T. Washington

Booker was a teacher. His school helped African Americans go to college, get good jobs, and start businesses.

What can people from the past teach us about helping others?

Sacagawea

Sacagawea was an explorer. Her skills helped other explorers cross the United States and make maps of the land.

MY TURN Interact with the text by writing a question you would ask one of these heroes.

_____

_____

_____

_____

Final Sounds

SEE and SAY Say each sound as you name each picture. Tell the final sound of each picture name.

Diphthongs oi, oy

The letters **oi** and **oy** make the vowel sound in **join** and **joy**.

MY TURN Read these words.

Diphthongs oi, oy

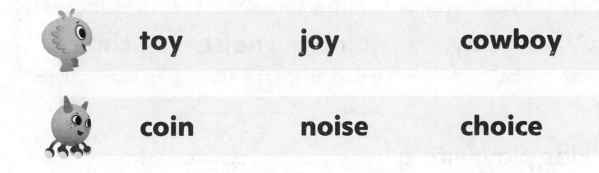

TURN and **TALK** Decode these words with a partner.

	toy	**joy**	**cowboy**
	coin	**noise**	**choice**

MY TURN Say the picture name. Write the letters that finish the word. Then read the word.

_oy

_oy

_oi

_oi

Diphthongs oi, oy

MY TURN Use a word from the box to finish each sentence. Then read the sentences.

toy	boy	join	noise	choice

The kids play with a _____toy_____.

Shh! It makes too much _____.

They make a _____ to go outside.

MY TURN Write your own sentences with the two words from the box that you did not use.

_____

_____

_____

_____

Initial and Final Sounds

SEE and SAY Say each sound as you name the pictures. Then say the picture names again.

Vowel Digraph ea

The letters **ea** can make the short **e** sound in **bread** or the long **e** sound in **bead.**

MY TURN Read these words. Try the long **e** sound and the short **e** sound.

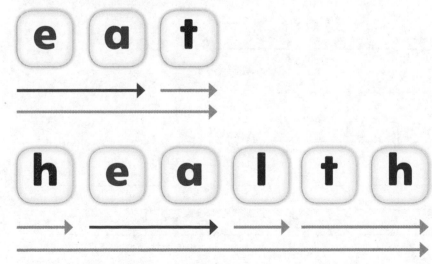

My Words to Know

Some words you must remember and practice.

MY TURN Read these words.

been	does	words	carry	going

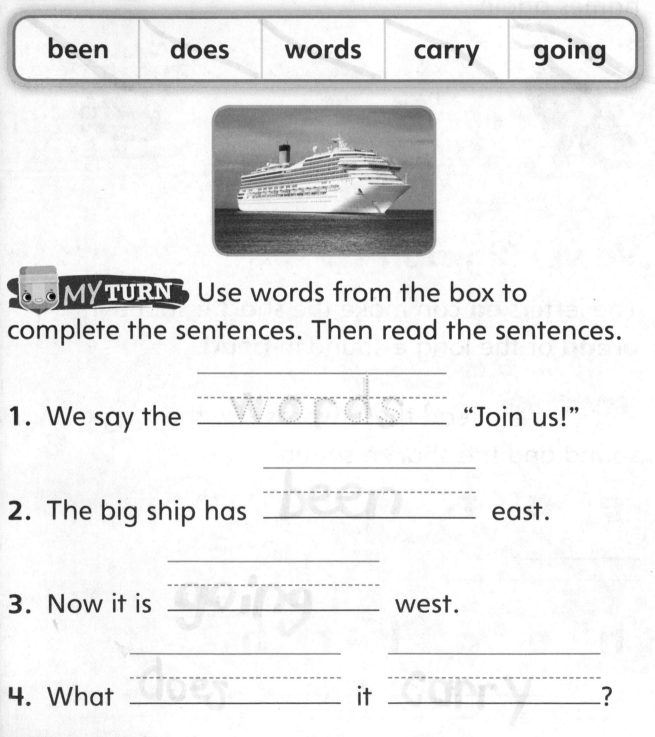

MY TURN Use words from the box to complete the sentences. Then read the sentences.

1. We say the _____words_____ "Join us!"

2. The big ship has _____been_____ east.

3. Now it is _____going_____ west.

4. What _____does_____ it _____carry_____?

Vowel Digraph ea

TURN and TALK Read these words.

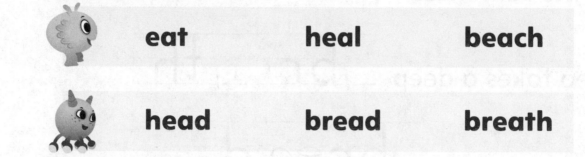

eat	heal	beach
head	bread	breath

MY TURN Say the picture names. Write the words. Sort for the long **e** or short **e** sound.

long e	short e
leaf	

Vowel Digraph ea

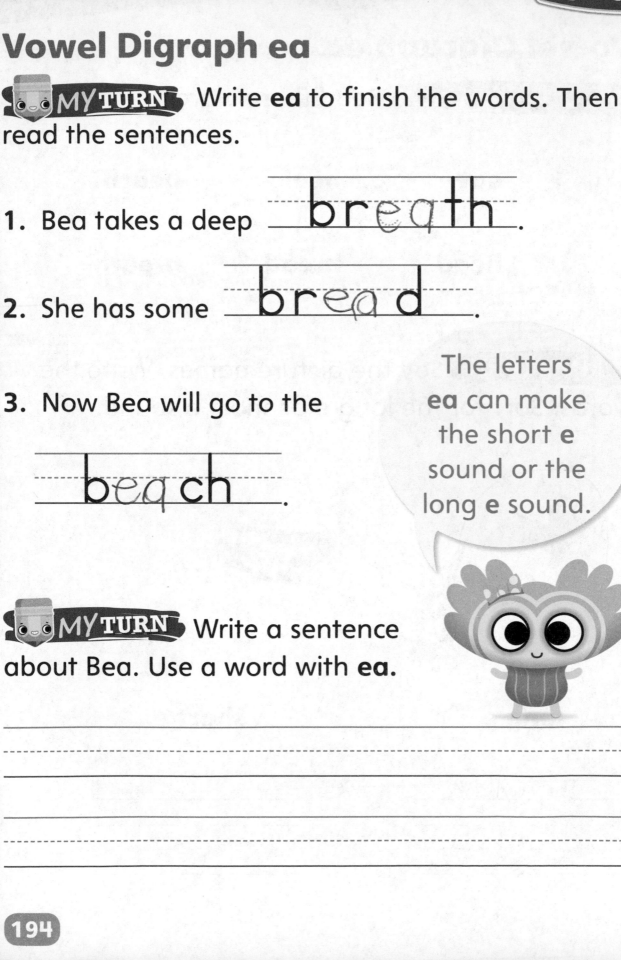 **MY TURN** Write **ea** to finish the words. Then read the sentences.

1. Bea takes a deep ___breath___.

2. She has some ___bread___.

3. Now Bea will go to the ___beach___.

> The letters **ea** can make the short **e** sound or the long **e** sound.

 **MY TURN** Write a sentence about Bea. Use a word with **ea**.

_____

_____

_____

_____

Nurse Joy

Joy gives her boy, Roy, some bread.

"What is your job?" he asks. Joy had been a head nurse.

What does a nurse do?

AUDIO

Audio with Highlighting

ANNOTATE

Highlight the two words with the short **e** sound spelled **ea**.

"Nurses heal," Joy said.

Roy likes those words.

Joy was glad to join a
team of nurses.

Underline the four words with the
same vowel sound as **toy** and **coin**.

A ship was going to carry her east.

She chose to leave and save lives.

"Mom is the best nurse!" Roy said.

Highlight the two words with the long **e** sound spelled **ea.**

My Learning Goal I can read a biography.

SPOTLIGHT ON GENRE

Biography

A biography has a main, or central, idea that tells what the text is mostly about.

Set a Purpose It is important to set a purpose, or reason, for reading. A purpose could be to learn about someone from the past. Setting a purpose helps readers understand more as they read a text.

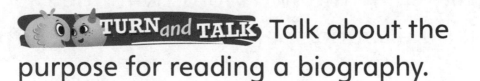 **TURN and TALK** Talk about the purpose for reading a biography.

Biography
Anchor Chart

The main idea of a biography is
what the text is mostly about.

Main idea:

Gail
has done
important
things in
her life.

Gail's Life
by Jack

Eleanor Roosevelt

Preview Vocabulary

You will read these vocabulary words in *Eleanor Roosevelt*.

| vote | views | rights | leaders |

Read

Read the title. Set a purpose for reading.

Ask questions about the text before reading.

Look at the photos and text together.

Talk about how this text answers the weekly question.

Meet the Author

Mathangi Subramanian writes about women and girls who change the world. She lives in New Delhi, India.

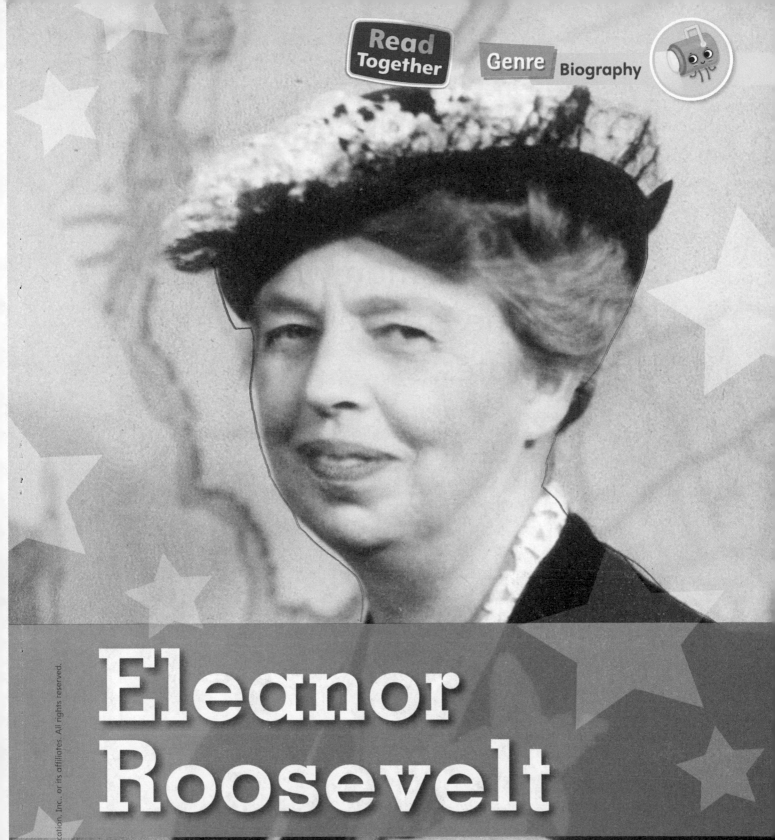

Eleanor Roosevelt

written by
Mathangi Subramanian

AUDIO

Audio with Highlighting

ANNOTATE

Eleanor Roosevelt had everything most people could want. She grew up in a wealthy family. She married a man who would become the President of the United States.

But Eleanor was not like most people. She wanted to be more than a President's wife. She wanted to help people.

CLOSE READ

<u>Underline</u> the main, or central, idea of this text.

Eleanor loved to travel. She traveled around the United States in trains. She liked meeting people and learning about them.

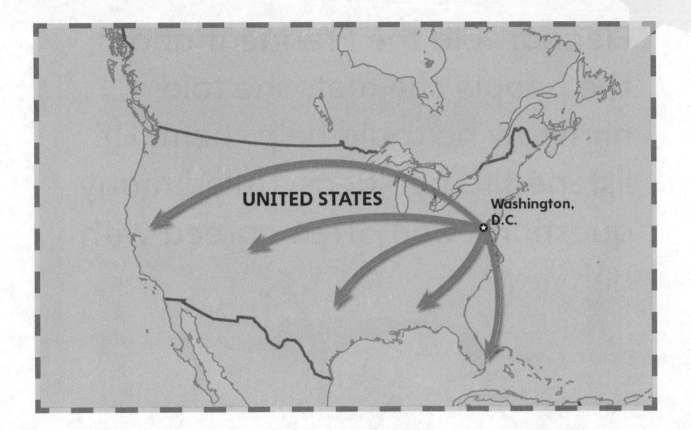

Eleanor visited farms, schools, and cities. Everywhere she went, she listened to the stories people told her about their lives.

VOCABULARY IN CONTEXT

Readers use clues in the words and pictures to figure out what an unfamiliar word means. Underline the words that help you figure out what **traveled** means.

Eleanor told the President about the people she met. She told him how he could help them. He listened to her ideas, asked many questions, and often agreed with her views.

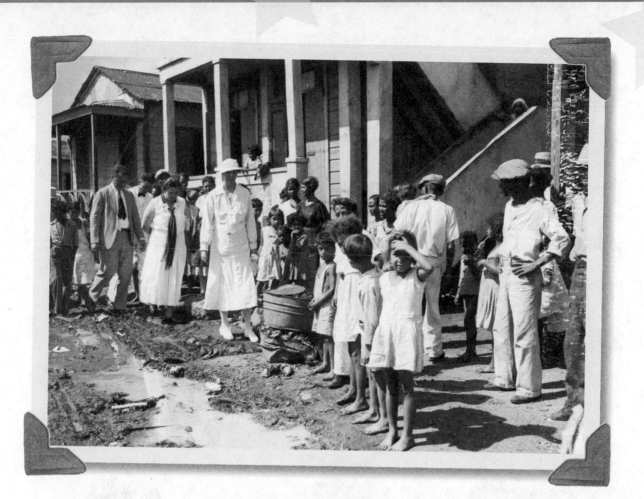

Eleanor met people who worked hard. They didn't have safe places to live. Eleanor helped them find homes.

CLOSE READ

How did Eleanor help people? Highlight the sentence that helps you answer this question.

Eleanor met women who wanted to do important things. She helped them get jobs and helped them become leaders. She helped them write stories for newspapers and magazines.

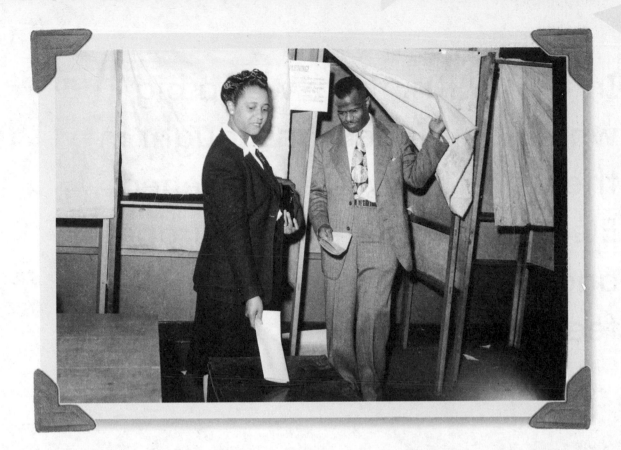

Eleanor met people who didn't get paid as much as others. In some places, they weren't allowed to vote. Eleanor helped them fight for their rights.

CLOSE READ

What question could you ask about how Eleanor helped people? Highlight the words that would answer the question.

In the 1940s, there was a big war. Many Americans fought in the war. They were frightened. Eleanor visited them in Europe and Asia. She helped them feel brave.

People loved Eleanor. She made the United States a better place. Learning about her might make you want to help people too.

CLOSE READ

Underline the sentence that tells a main, or central, idea of the text.

Develop Vocabulary

MY TURN Look at each picture. <u>Underline</u> the vocabulary word that completes the sentence.

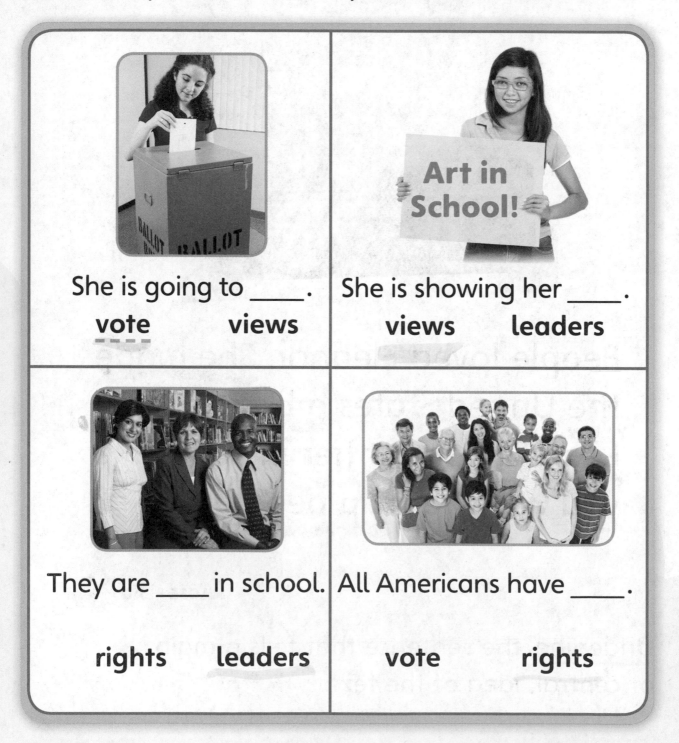

She is going to ____.
vote   views

She is showing her ____.
views   leaders

They are ____ in school.

rights   leaders

All Americans have ____.

vote   rights

Check for Understanding

MY TURN Write the answers to the questions. You can look back at the text.

1. How do you know this text is a biography?

_____

_____

----

2. Why does the author use photographs?

_____

_____

----

3. How were Eleanor and President Roosevelt similar? Use text evidence.

_____

_____

Find the Main Idea

The **main**, or **central**, **idea** is what a text is mostly about. **Supporting evidence** is the details that tell more about the main idea.

MY TURN What is the main idea of *Eleanor Roosevelt?* Go back to what you underlined in the text to help you answer.

The main, or central, idea is

_____

_____

_____

_____

_____

What supporting evidence supports the main idea?

_____

_____

_____

_____

Ask and Answer Questions

Readers generate questions before, during, and after reading to better understand and learn about the main, or central, idea. They can use the details in the text to find answers.

MY TURN Write a question you had while reading *Eleanor Roosevelt*. Look back at what you highlighted in the text.

_____

_____

_____

_____

_____

_____

TURN and TALK After reading the text, ask a partner additional questions you have. Asking questions will help you learn more.

Reflect and Share

Write to Sources

You have read about different people from the past. On a separate sheet of paper, write comments about how these people are similar and different.

Making Comments

When writing comments about texts, it is important to use text evidence. You should:

- Find examples that support your ideas.
- Use examples from both texts.

Weekly Question

What can people from the past teach us about helping others?

I can make and use words to read and write narrative nonfiction.

My Learning Goal

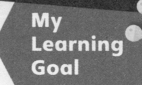

Academic Vocabulary

MY TURN Draw a line to match the person you read about in this unit to the sentence that describes him or her.

Jackie Robinson

Painting was how she **recorded** her **experiences.**

Georgia O'Keeffe

Many people think she **supplied** our country with its first American flag.

Betsy Ross

He helped make **necessary** changes in baseball.

Read Like a Writer, Write for a Reader

A **third-person text** is told by someone who is not a part of the text. Third-person texts use words such as **he**, **she**, **it**, or **they**.

> Eleanor loved to travel. She traveled around the United States in trains.

◁ ········ The author uses these words to help readers understand that the story is a third-person text.

MY TURN Write sentences about another person. Use words to show it is a third-person text.

_____

_____

_____

_____

_____

_____

_____

_____

Spell Words with Diphthongs oi, oy

The letters **oi** and **oy** spell the sound you hear in **join** and **boy**. A **dictionary** tells the meanings and spellings of words.

MY TURN Sort and spell the words. Find four words in a dictionary.

oi	oy
boil	boy

My Words to Know

Spelling Words

boy

join

spoil

boil

coin

toy

soil

joy

My Words to Know

going

been

Compound Sentences

A compound sentence is two simple sentences joined by a comma and a conjunction. Some conjunctions are **and**, **so**, and **but**.

She traveled. She met people.
She traveled, **and** she met people.

MY TURN Edit these simple sentences to make one compound sentence.

1. They needed help. She helped them.

_____

- -

_____

- -

_____

2. What can we do? How can we help?

_____

- -

_____

- -

_____

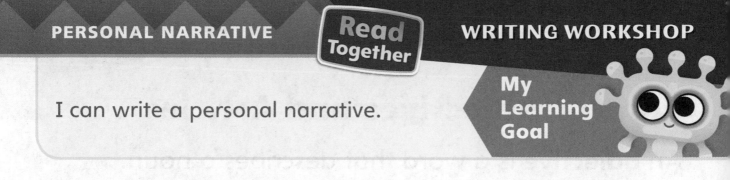

I can write a personal narrative.

Edit for Pronouns

A **pronoun** takes the place of a noun.

Subjective pronouns: I, you, she, he, it, we, they

Objective pronouns: me, you, him, her, us, them

Possessive pronouns: mine, yours, ours, hers, his

MY TURN Edit these sentences by writing the pronoun that can replace the underlined words.

1. <u>Jake</u> was hungry. _____He_____

2. I will make a snack for <u>Jake</u>. _____

3. The snack was <u>Jake's</u>. _____

MY TURN Edit the pronouns in your personal narrative draft.

Edit for Adjectives and Articles

An **adjective** is a word that describes a noun.
The article **the** tells about a specific noun.
The articles **a** and **an** tell about any noun.
The words **this, that, these,** and **those** tell which
one or which ones. **This** and **that** tell about singular
nouns. **These** and **those** tell about plural nouns.

MY TURN Edit these sentences by adding adjectives and articles.

1. I need _____ a new _____ book for class.

2. I want to write _____ story.

3. Will I need _____ book?

MY TURN Edit the adjectives and articles in your personal narrative.

Assessment

You have learned how to write a personal narrative.

MY TURN Read the list. Put a check next to what you can do.

I can generate an idea to plan a narrative.	☐
I can choose a setting.	☐
I can write about me as the narrator.	☐
I can write a problem and resolution.	☐
I can write what happens first, next, and last.	☐
I can edit for capitalization and punctuation.	☐
I can edit for verbs, pronouns, adjectives, and articles.	☐

UNIT THEME
Making History

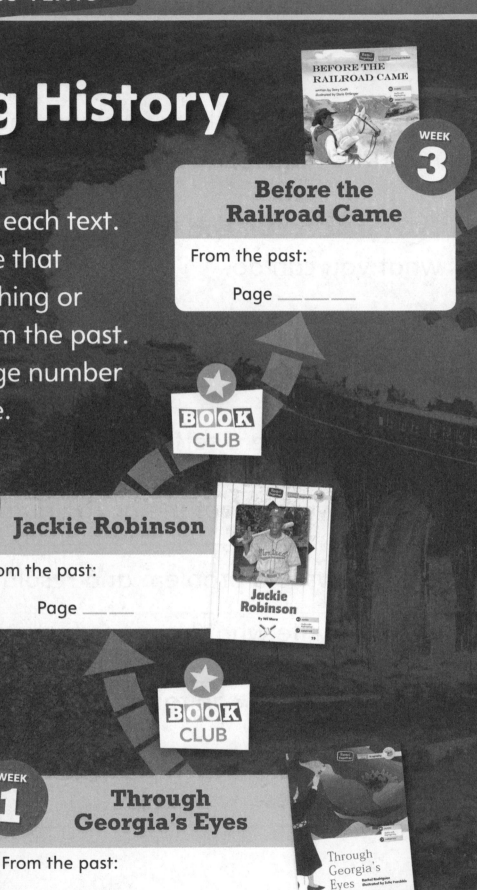

MY TURN

Look back at each text. Find a picture that shows something or someone from the past. Write the page number of the picture.

WEEK 3

BEFORE THE RAILROAD CAME

written by Jerry Craft
illustrated by Doris Ettlinger

Before the Railroad Came

From the past:

Page _____ _____

★ BOOK CLUB

WEEK 2

Jackie Robinson

From the past:

Page _____

Jackie Robinson
By Wil Mara
79

★ BOOK CLUB

WEEK 1

Through Georgia's Eyes

From the past:

Page _____

Through Georgia's Eyes
Rachel Rodriguez
Illustrated by Julie Paschkis
27

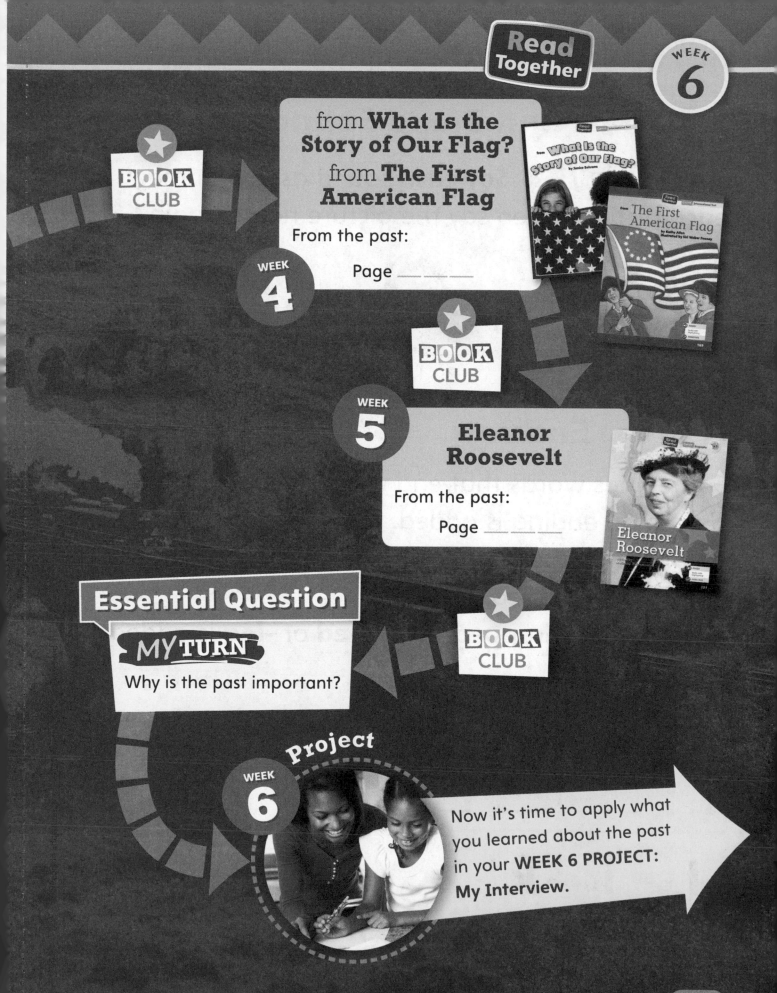

from **What Is the Story of Our Flag?**
from **The First American Flag**

BOOK CLUB

From the past:

Page _____ _____ _____

WEEK
4

BOOK CLUB

WEEK
5

Eleanor Roosevelt

From the past:

Page _____ _____ _____

Essential Question

MY TURN

Why is the past important?

BOOK CLUB

Project

WEEK
6

Now it's time to apply what you learned about the past in your **WEEK 6 PROJECT:** **My Interview.**

Segment and Blend Sounds

 **SEE and SAY** Say each sound as you name each picture. Then say the picture name again.

Adding Endings

Sometimes words that end with **y** or **e** change before an ending is added.

The final **y** becomes the letter **i** before **-es** or **-ed** is added.

The final **e** is dropped before **-ed** or **-ing** is added.

MY TURN Read these words.

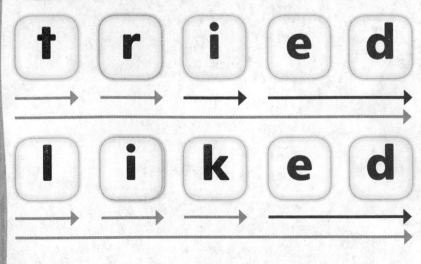

Adding Endings

 **TURN and TALK** Read these words with a partner.

tries	dried	shaking

liked	ladies	waving

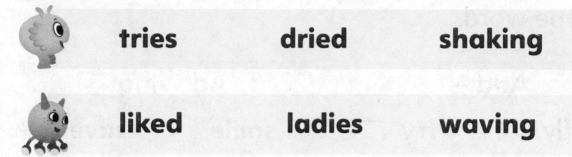 **MY TURN** Add the ending to each word. Write the word. Then read the words.

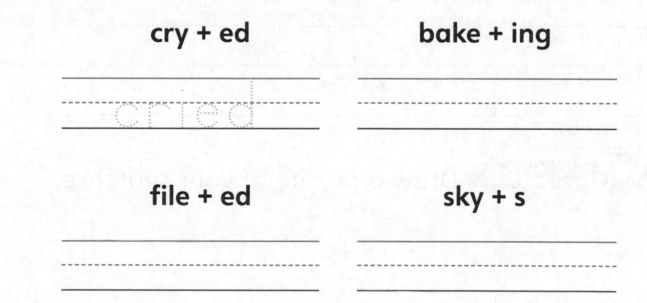

cry + ed

cried

bake + ing

file + ed

sky + s

Adding Endings

MY TURN Choose one of the words below. Add the ending to the word. Then write a sentence using the word.

Add -s		Add -ing	
fly	try	smile	wave

_____

- -

_____

- -

_____

- -

_____

MY TURN Draw a picture of your sentence.

Read Together

Spell Words with Endings

Base words can change **y** to **i** or drop final **-e** before adding the ending.

MY TURN Sort and spell the words.

Spelling Words

baby	city	cities	living
babies	giving	having	baking

No Ending

baby

Change y to i

Drop Final -e

My Words to Know

give   right

Middle and Final Sounds

 **SEE** *and* **SAY** Say each sound as you name the pictures. Then say the picture names again.

Vowel Team ie

The letters **ie** can make the long **i** sound in **tie** or the long **e** sound in **piece**.

MY TURN Read the words. Try the long **e** sound. Then try the long **i** sound.

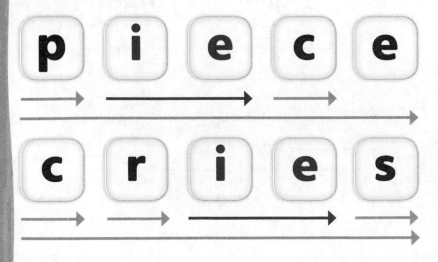

p i e c e

c r i e s

My Words to Know

Some words you must remember and practice.

MY TURN Read these words.

may	give	right	other	number

MY TURN Use the words in the box to complete the sentences. Then read the sentences.

1. Mom bakes a _number_ of pies.

2. She says I _____ take one piece.

3. I will get it _____ now.

4. Mom will _____ the _____ pie to her niece.

Vowel Team ie

TURN and TALK Decode these words with a partner. Tell which vowel sound you hear.

| brief | piece | shield | chief |

| dried | skies | flies | tried |

MY TURN Choose a word that has the long **e** or long **i** sound spelled **ie**. Write the word and draw a picture showing the word.

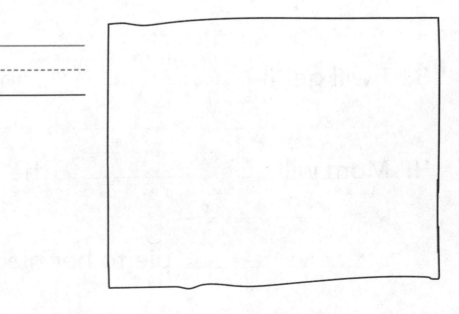

_____

- - - - - - - - - - - - - - -

_____

Vowel Team ie

MY TURN Write **ie**. Read the words. Match the word to the picture it names.

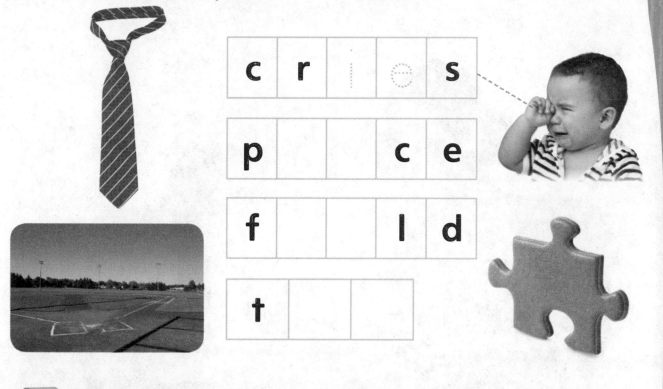

c	r	i	e	s

p			c	e

f			l	d

t		

MY TURN Write a sentence using a word with the vowel team **ie**.

_____

- -

_____

- -

_____

- -

_____

A Piece of the Past

 AUDIO

Audio with
Highlighting

ANNOTATE

Mom tells me what her past was like.

She points to a number of pages.

For a brief time she danced.

Mom baked pumpkin pie too!

Read the title and story. Underline the three words with the vowel team **ie**.

Mom points to the other page.

"On the right side, I am riding.

I tried making the team.

I cried when I didn't."

Highlight the two words that change
y to **i** before adding an ending.

I <u>smiled</u> at Mom.

"I like your page for riding,"
I said.

"I may give dancing a try!"

<u>Underline</u> the three words that drop
final **-e** before adding an ending.

MY Interview

Activity

Interview an older person about someone who was important to them. Write about the interview in an essay.

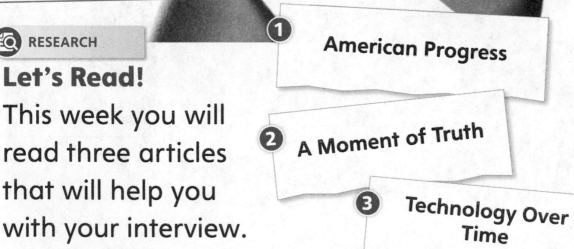

RESEARCH

Let's Read!

This week you will read three articles that will help you with your interview.

1 American Progress

2 A Moment of Truth

3 Technology Over Time

 **COLLABORATE** Researchers think of questions they want to have answered. Who will you interview? Generate questions to ask that person.

Use Academic Words

COLLABORATE Talk about the picture with your partner. Use the academic words.

COLLABORATE When we research something, we develop, or make, a plan. Then we follow the steps. With a partner, develop and follow a research plan.

Interview Research Plan

☐ Ask questions.

☐ ----------------------------------

☐ ----------------------------------

☐ ----------------------------------

☐ ----------------------------------

Inform Readers

Some authors write to inform readers about a topic. When reading informational text, look for a main, or central, idea and supporting evidence, or details.

COLLABORATE Read "A Moment of Truth" with a partner. Then fill in the chart.

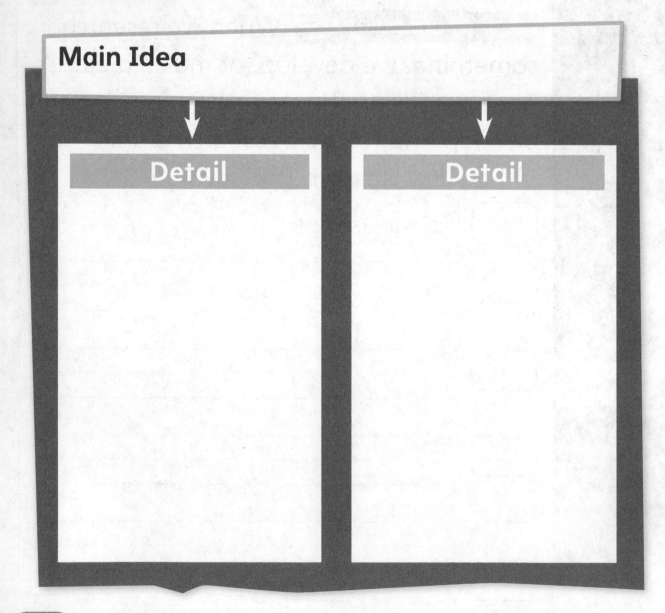

Main Idea

Detail

Detail

Any Questions?

An **interview** is when one person asks questions and another person answers them. Introduce yourself to the person you interview.

I will interview _____

I will ask _____

_____

COLLABORATE (Circle) how you will gather information from the person you interview.

Record   **Write**

Informational Essay

Informational essays include a title, a main idea, and details. The information can be organized in a way that describes the topic.

Mr. Kwan and His Friend Joe — Title

Mr. Kwan's best friend was — Main Idea
named Joe. Joe lived next to
Mr. Kwan. They walked home
from school together. Then
they played with their yo-yos
in Mr. Kwan's backyard. — Details
Mr. Kwan and Joe are still
friends today!

Take Notes

COLLABORATE Follow these tips for taking notes during your interview.

1 Write your questions before the interview.

2 Add space so you can write responses.

3 Write important words and phrases instead of sentences.

My Interview Questions

1. Who was your best friend?

2. What did you like to do together?

COLLABORATE Write something you learned about the person you interviewed.

I learned that _____

Thank You!

After your interview, write a note to thank the person you interviewed. Begin your note with **Dear** and the person's name. End your note with **Sincerely** or **Your friend** and your name.

Dear Mr. Kwan,

Thank you for the interview. I liked

your stories.

Your friend, Ben

COLLABORATE Complete the thank-you note.

Dear _____,

Thank you for _____

_____.

Sincerely, _____

Revise

 COLLABORATE Read your essay to your partner.

Did you check your

title?	yes	no
main, or central, idea?	yes	no
details?	yes	no

> Did you use details that support the main idea?

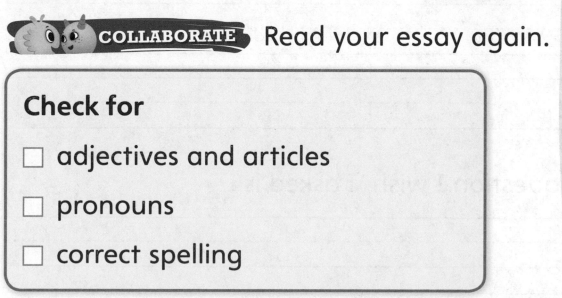

Edit

 COLLABORATE Read your essay again.

Check for

- ☐ adjectives and articles
- ☐ pronouns
- ☐ correct spelling

Share

COLLABORATE Share your essay with the class.

Follow the rules for **speaking and listening**.

- Speak clearly at a good pace.
- Take turns speaking.
- Answer questions in complete sentences.

Reflect

MY TURN Complete the sentences.

My favorite part about doing the interview is

_____

_____

_____

One question I wish I asked is

_____

_____

_____

Reflect on Your Goals

Look back at your unit goals. Use a different color to rate yourself again.

MY TURN Complete the sentences.

Reflect on Your Reading

One thing I like about a book I chose on my own is

_____

_____

Reflect on Writing

One skill I want to work on is

_____

_____

How to Use a Picture Dictionary

You can use a picture dictionary to find words. The words are grouped into topics. The topic of this picture dictionary is **sequence**. Look at the pictures, and try to read the words. The pictures will help you understand the meanings of the words.

This is the word you are learning.

This is a picture of the word.

beginning

 TURNand**TALK** Find the word **end** in the picture dictionary. Use the word **end** to tell about your day.

Sequence

before

after

beginning

end

first

next

then

last

Read Together

How to Use a Digital Resource

An online dictionary, or **digital resource,** can help you find the meanings of words that are not in this glossary. Type the word you are looking for in the search box. When you hit return, the word and meaning will pop up.

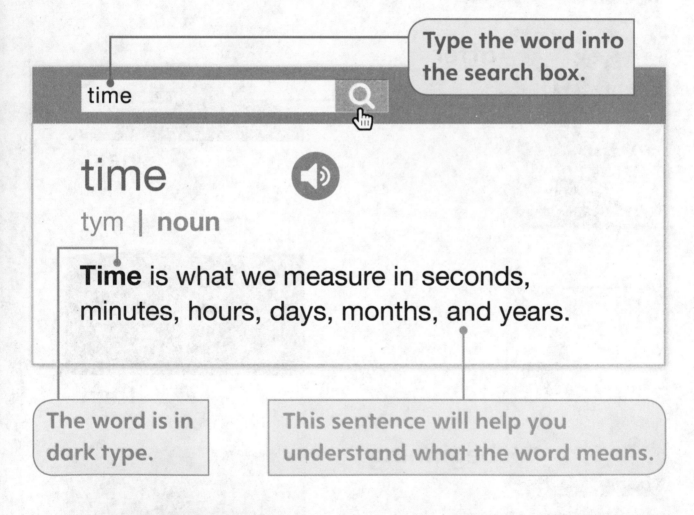

Type the word into the search box.

time

time 🔊

tym | **noun**

Time is what we measure in seconds, minutes, hours, days, months, and years.

The word is in dark type.

This sentence will help you understand what the word means.

TURN and TALK Use a digital resource to find the word **tradition.** To be sure you understand what the word means, use the word in a few sentences.

Aa

admired If you **admired** someone, you thought highly of that person.

allowed If something is **allowed**, it is permitted to happen.

amaze If things **amaze** you, they fill you with wonder.

Cc

cattle **Cattle** is a group of cows, bulls, and steers.

cheered If a group **cheered**, they yelled support or praise.

Dd

discovers When someone **discovers** something, he or she finds or sees it for the first time.

drive A **drive** is an organized way of directing animals to move.

Ee

experience An **experience** is something a person has seen, done, or lived through.

Ff

field A **field** is an area where information is placed.

Ll

leaders **Leaders** are the people in charge.

loved If a person **loved** something, he or she liked it very much.

Mm

memory A **memory** is a person, thing, or event that you can remember.

Nn

necessary If something is **necessary**, it needs to be done.

Pp

patch A **patch** is a small area that is different from the surrounding area.

railroad • rights

Rr

railroad A **railroad** is the steel tracks that trains travel on.

ranch A **ranch** is a very large farm.

record When you **record** information, you write something so that it can be used in the future.

rights **Rights** are things that a person is allowed to have, get, or do.

Ss

stars **Stars** are shapes that have five or more points.

stripes **Stripes** are lines that are different colors.

supply When you **supply** something, you provide what is needed.

Vv

views A person's **views** are the way he or she thinks about something. Views are an opinion.

vote When you **vote**, you decide something or choose someone by making a choice.

Ww

wonder When you **wonder**, you are curious about something.